D0009444

[illegible]ND CARVER'S

[illegible] TALK ABOUT

[illegible]K ABOUT LOVE

[illegible]orary writer of short stories than [illegible] Perhaps a handful as good, but none bet- [illegible]ly 200 years ago, Wordsworth and Coleridge st[illegible]ed a revolution when they proclaimed their aim to write in 'the language really used by men.' Neither of them quite achieved that. In [this collection], Raymond Carver has. And it is terrifying." —Robert Houston, *The Nation*

"In Raymond Carver's stories, it is dangerous even to speak. Conversation completes the damage people have already done to one another in silence. It is not safe to form a sentence or even to speak a name. To say 'Duane' or 'Holly' is to pronounce yet another doom. This is the fiction Carver writes, and I know of nothing stronger in its kind."

—Denis Donoghue

"Masterful. . . . The first impact of all the stories is sharp and visceral. Only afterward, as the skeleton of each one keeps rattling in the mind, does the painstaking intelligence of their designer become apparent."

—Meredith Marsh, *New Republic*

"I'm nuts about Raymond Carver's new stories. They're real as discount stores, time clocks, the franchises in small towns, bad marriages. His rumpled men and ragged women will break your heart." —Stanley Elkin

"A book of fables for this decade."

—Jayne Anne Phillips, *New York*

BOOKS BY RAYMOND CARVER

FICTION

Where I'm Calling From
Will You Please Be Quiet, Please?
Furious Seasons
What We Talk About When We Talk About Love
Cathedral

POETRY

A New Path to the Waterfall
Winter Insomnia
At Night the Salmon Move
Where Water Comes Together with Other Water
Ultramarine

PROSE AND POETRY

No Heroics, Please
Fires

WHAT WE TALK ABOUT WHEN WE TALK ABOUT LOVE

1502
9.30

C
813
C331wh

STORIES BY

WHAT WE TALK ABOUT WHEN WE TALK ABOUT LOVE

RAYMOND CARVER

Christian Heritage
College Library
2100 Greenfield Dr.
El Cajon, CA 92019

VINTAGE CONTEMPORARIES · VINTAGE BOOKS

A DIVISION OF RANDOM HOUSE, INC. · NEW YORK

78138

Vintage Books Edition, June 1989
Copyright ©1974, 1976, 1978, 1980, 1981 by Raymond Carver

All rights reserved under International and Pan-American Copyright Conventions. Published in the United States by Random House, Inc., New York, and simultaneously in Canada by Random House of Canada Limited, Toronto. Originally published in hardcover by Alfred A. Knopf, Inc., New York, in April 1981 and in softcover by Vintage Books, a division of Random House, Inc., in March 1982.

Most of the stories in this work have been previously published in *Antaeus, The Iowa Review, The Missouri Review, New England Review, North American Review, The Paris Review, Perspective, Quarterly West,* and *Tri-Quarterly.*

"So Much Water So Close To Home," "Everything Stuck to Him" (originally "Distance"), and "The Third Thing That Killed My Father Off" (originally "Dummy") are from *Furious Seasons,* copyright ©1977 by Raymond Carver. Reprinted by permission of Capra Press, Santa Barbara.

Library of Congress Cataloging-in-Publication Data
Carver, Raymond.
What we talk about when we talk about love.
I. Title.
PS3553.A7894W4 1982 813'.54 81-52447
ISBN 0-679-72305-6 (pbk.) AACR2

Display typography by Stephanie Bart-Horvath

Manufactured in the United States of America
9B

FOR TESS GALLAGHER

The author is pleased to acknowledge receipt of a John Simon Guggenheim Memorial Fellowship and a National Endowment for the Arts grant. He also wishes to express grateful acknowledgment and appreciation to Noel Young of Capra Press.

Contents

WHAT WE TALK ABOUT WHEN WE TALK ABOUT LOVE

Why Don't You Dance?

IN the kitchen, he poured another drink and looked at the bedroom suite in his front yard. The mattress was stripped and the candy-striped sheets lay beside two pillows on the chiffonier. Except for that, things looked much the way they had in the bedroom—nightstand and reading lamp on his side of the bed, nightstand and reading lamp on her side.

His side, her side.

He considered this as he sipped the whiskey.

The chiffonier stood a few feet from the foot of the bed. He had emptied the drawers into cartons that morning, and the cartons were in the living room. A portable heater was next to the chiffonier. A rattan chair with a decorator pillow stood at the foot of the bed. The buffed aluminum kitchen set took up a part of the driveway. A yellow muslin cloth, much too large, a gift, covered the table and hung down over the sides. A potted fern was on the table, along with a box of silverware and a record player, also gifts. A big console-model television set rested on a coffee table, and a few feet away from this stood a sofa and chair and a floor lamp. The desk was pushed against the garage door. A few utensils were on the desk, along with a wall clock and two framed prints. There was also in the driveway a carton with cups, glasses, and plates, each object wrapped in newspaper. That morning he had cleared out the closets, and except for the three cartons in the living room, all the stuff was out of the house. He had run an extension cord on out there and everything was connected. Things worked, no different from how it was when they were inside.

Now and then a car slowed and people stared. But no one stopped.

It occurred to him that he wouldn't, either.

"IT must be a yard sale," the girl said to the boy.

This girl and this boy were furnishing a little apartment.

"Let's see what they want for the bed," the girl said.

"And for the TV," the boy said.

The boy pulled into the driveway and stopped in front of the kitchen table.

They got out of the car and began to examine things, the girl touching the muslin cloth, the boy plugging in the blender and turning the dial to MINCE, the girl picking up a chafing dish, the boy turning on the television set and making little adjustments.

He sat down on the sofa to watch. He lit a cigarette,

looked around, flipped the match into the grass.

The girl sat on the bed. She pushed off her shoes and lay back. She thought she could see a star.

"Come here, Jack. Try this bed. Bring one of those pillows," she said.

"How is it?" he said.

"Try it," she said.

He looked around. The house was dark.

"I feel funny," he said. "Better see if anybody's home."

She bounced on the bed.

"Try it first," she said.

He lay down on the bed and put the pillow under his head.

"How does it feel?" she said.

"It feels firm," he said.

She turned on her side and put her hand to his face.

"Kiss me," she said.

"Let's get up," he said.

"Kiss me," she said.

She closed her eyes. She held him.

He said, "I'll see if anybody's home."

But he just sat up and stayed where he was, making believe he was watching the television.

Lights came on in houses up and down the street.

"Wouldn't it be funny if," the girl said and grinned and didn't finish.

The boy laughed, but for no good reason. For no good reason, he switched the reading lamp on.

The girl brushed away a mosquito, whereupon the boy stood up and tucked in his shirt.

"I'll see if anybody's home," he said. "I don't think anybody's home. But if anybody is, I'll see what things are going for."

"Whatever they ask, offer ten dollars less. It's always a good idea," she said. "And, besides, they must be desperate or something."

"It's a pretty good TV," the boy said.

"Ask them how much," the girl said.

THE man came down the sidewalk with a sack from the market. He had sandwiches, beer, whiskey. He saw the car in the driveway and the girl on the bed. He saw the television set going and the boy on the porch.

"Hello," the man said to the girl. "You found the bed. That's good."

"Hello," the girl said, and got up. "I was just trying it out." She patted the bed. "It's a pretty good bed."

"It's a good bed," the man said, and put down the sack and took out the beer and the whiskey.

"We thought nobody was here," the boy said. "We're interested in the bed and maybe in the TV. Also maybe the desk. How much do you want for the bed?"

"I was thinking fifty dollars for the bed," the man said.

"Would you take forty?" the girl asked.

"I'll take forty," the man said.

He took a glass out of the carton. He took the newspaper off the glass. He broke the seal on the whiskey.

"How about the TV?" the boy said.

"Twenty-five."

"Would you take fifteen?" the girl said.

"Fifteen's okay. I could take fifteen," the man said.

The girl looked at the boy.

"You kids, you'll want a drink," the man said. "Glasses in that box. I'm going to sit down. I'm going to sit down on the sofa."

The man sat on the sofa, leaned back, and stared at the boy and the girl.

THE boy found two glasses and poured whiskey.

"That's enough," the girl said. "I think I want water in mine."

She pulled out a chair and sat at the kitchen table.

"There's water in that spigot over there," the man said. "Turn on that spigot."

The boy came back with the watered whiskey. He cleared his throat and sat down at the kitchen table. He grinned. But he didn't drink anything from his glass.

The man gazed at the television. He finished his drink and started another. He reached to turn on the floor lamp. It was then that his cigarette dropped from his fingers and fell between the cushions.

The girl got up to help him find it.

"So what do you want?" the boy said to the girl.

The boy took out the checkbook and held it to his lips as if thinking.

"I want the desk," the girl said. "How much money is the desk?"

The man waved his hand at this preposterous question.

"Name a figure," he said.

He looked at them as they sat at the table. In the lamplight, there was something about their faces. It was nice or it was nasty. There was no telling.

"I'M going to turn off this TV and put on a record," the man said. "This record-player is going, too. Cheap. Make me an offer."

He poured more whiskey and opened a beer.

"Everything goes," said the man.

The girl held out her glass and the man poured.

"Thank you," she said. "You're very nice," she said.

"It goes to your head," the boy said. "I'm getting it in the head." He held up his glass and jiggled it.

The man finished his drink and poured another, and then he found the box with the records.

"Pick something," the man said to the girl, and he held the records out to her.

The boy was writing the check.

"Here," the girl said, picking something, picking anything, for she did not know the names on these labels. She got up from the table and sat down again. She did not want to sit still.

"I'm making it out to cash," the boy said.

"Sure," the man said.

They drank. They listened to the record. And then the man put on another.

Why don't you kids dance? he decided to say, and then he said it. "Why don't you dance?"

"I don't think so," the boy said.

"Go ahead," the man said. "It's my yard. You can dance if you want to."

ARMS about each other, their bodies pressed together, the boy and the girl moved up and down the driveway. They were dancing. And when the record was over, they did it again, and when that one ended, the boy said, "I'm drunk."

The girl said, "You're not drunk."

"Well, I'm drunk," the boy said.

The man turned the record over and the boy said, "I am."

"Dance with me," the girl said to the boy and then to the man, and when the man stood up, she came to him with her arms wide open.

"THOSE people over there, they're watching," she said.

"It's okay," the man said. "It's my place," he said.

"Let them watch," the girl said.

"That's right," the man said. "They thought they'd seen everything over here. But they haven't seen this, have they?" he said.

He felt her breath on his neck.

"I hope you like your bed," he said.

The girl closed and then opened her eyes. She pushed her face into the man's shoulder. She pulled the man closer.

"You must be desperate or something," she said.

WEEKS later, she said: "The guy was about middle-aged. All his things right there in his yard. No lie. We got real pissed and danced. In the driveway. Oh, my God. Don't laugh. He played us these records. Look at this record-player. The old guy gave it to us. And all these crappy records. Will you look at this shit?"

She kept talking. She told everyone. There was more to it, and she was trying to get it talked out. After a time, she quit trying.

Viewfinder

A MAN without hands came to the door to sell me a photograph of my house. Except for the chrome hooks, he was an ordinary-looking man of fifty or so.

"How did you lose your hands?" I asked after he'd said what he wanted.

"That's another story," he said. "You want this picture or not?"

"Come in," I said. "I just made coffee."

I'd just made some Jell-O, too. But I didn't tell the man I did.

"I might use your toilet," the man with no hands said.

I wanted to see how he would hold a cup.

I knew how he held the camera. It was an old Polaroid,

big and black. He had it fastened to leather straps that looped over his shoulders and went around his back, and it was this that secured the camera to his chest. He would stand on the sidewalk in front of your house, locate your house in the viewfinder, push down the lever with one of his hooks, and out would pop your picture.

I'd been watching from the window, you see.

"WHERE did you say the toilet was?"

"Down there, turn right."

Bending, hunching, he let himself out of the straps. He put the camera on the sofa and straightened his jacket.

"You can look at this while I'm gone."

I took the picture from him.

There was a little rectangle of lawn, the driveway, the carport, front steps, bay window, and the window I'd been watching from in the kitchen.

So why would I want a photograph of this tragedy?

I looked a little closer and saw my head, *my head*, in there inside the kitchen window.

It made me think, seeing myself like that. I can tell you, it makes a man think.

I heard the toilet flush. He came down the hall, zipping and smiling, one hook holding his belt, the other tucking in his shirt.

"What do you think?" he said. "All right? Personally, I think it turned out fine. Don't I know what I'm doing? Let's face it, it takes a professional."

He plucked at his crotch.

"Here's coffee," I said.

He said, "You're alone, right?"

He looked at the living room. He shook his head.

"Hard, hard," he said.

He sat next to the camera, leaned back with a sigh, and smiled as if he knew something he wasn't going to tell me.

"Drink your coffee," I said.

I WAS trying to think of something to say.

"Three kids were by here wanting to paint my address on the curb. They wanted a dollar to do it. You wouldn't know anything about that, would you?"

It was a long shot. But I watched him just the same.

He leaned forward importantly, the cup balanced between his hooks. He set it down on the table.

"I work alone," he said. "Always have, always will. What are you saying?" he said.

"I was trying to make a connection," I said.

I had a headache. I know coffee's no good for it, but sometimes Jell-O helps. I picked up the picture.

"I was in the kitchen," I said. "Usually I'm in the back."

"Happens all the time," he said. "So they just up and left you, right? Now you take me, I work alone. So what do you say? You want the picture?"

"I'll take it," I said.

I stood up and picked up the cups.

"Sure you will," he said. "Me, I keep a room downtown. It's okay. I take a bus out, and after I've worked the neighborhoods, I go to another downtown. You see what I'm saying? Hey, I had kids once. Just like you," he said.

I waited with the cups and watched him struggle up from the sofa.

He said, "They're what gave me this."

I took a good look at those hooks.

"Thanks for the coffee and the use of the toilet. I sympathize."

He raised and lowered his hooks.

"Show me," I said. "Show me how much. Take more pictures of me and my house."

"It won't work," the man said. "They're not coming back."

But I helped him get into his straps.

"I can give you a rate," he said. "Three for a dollar." He said, "If I go any lower, I don't come out."

WE went outside. He adjusted the shutter. He told me where to stand, and we got down to it.

We moved around the house. Systematic. Sometimes I'd look sideways. Sometimes I'd look straight ahead.

"Good," he'd say. "That's good," he'd say, until we'd circled the house and were back in the front again. "That's twenty. That's enough."

"No," I said. "On the roof," I said.

"Jesus," he said. He checked up and down the block. "Sure," he said. "Now you're talking."

I said, "The whole kit and kaboodle. They cleared right out."

"Look at this!" the man said, and again he held up his hooks.

I WENT inside and got a chair. I put it up under the carport. But it didn't reach. So I got a crate and put the crate on top of the chair.

It was okay up there on the roof.

I stood up and looked around. I waved, and the man with no hands waved back with his hooks.

It was then I saw them, the rocks. It was like a little rock nest on the screen over the chimney hole. You know kids. You know how they lob them up, thinking to sink one down your chimney.

"Ready?" I called, and I got a rock, and I waited until he had me in his viewfinder.

"Okay!" he called.

I laid back my arm and I hollered, "Now!" I threw that son of a bitch as far as I could throw it.

"I don't know," I heard him shout. "I don't do motion shots."

"Again!" I screamed, and took up another rock.

Mr. Coffee and Mr. Fixit

I'VE seen some things. I was going over to my mother's to stay a few nights. But just as I got to the top of the stairs, I looked and she was on the sofa kissing a man. It was summer. The door was open. The TV was going. That's one of the things I've seen.

My mother is sixty-five. She belongs to a singles club. Even so, it was hard. I stood with my hand on the railing and watched as the man kissed her. She was kissing him back, and the TV was going.

Things are better now. But back in those days, when my mother was putting out, I was out of work. My kids were crazy, and my wife was crazy. She was putting out too. The guy that was getting it was an unemployed aerospace engineer she'd met at AA. He was also crazy.

His name was Ross and he had six kids. He walked with a limp from a gunshot wound his first wife gave him.

I don't know what we were thinking of in those days.

This guy's second wife had come and gone, but it was his first wife who had shot him for not meeting his payments. I wish him well now. Ross. What a name! But it was different then. In those days I mentioned weapons. I'd say to my wife, "I think I'll get a Smith and Wesson." But I never did it.

Ross was a little guy. But not too little. He had a moustache and always wore a button-up sweater.

His one wife jailed him once. The second one did. I found out from my daughter that my wife went bail. My daughter Melody didn't like it any better than I did. About the bail. It wasn't that Melody was looking out for me. She wasn't looking out for either one of us, her mother or me neither. It was just that there was a serious cash thing and if some of it went to Ross, there'd be that much less for Melody. So Ross was on Melody's list. Also, she didn't like his kids, and his having so many of them. But in general Melody said Ross was all right.

He'd even told her fortune once.

THIS Ross guy spent his time repairing things, now that he had no regular job. But I'd seen his house from the outside. It was a mess. Junk all around. Two busted Plymouths in the yard.

In the first stages of the thing they had going, my wife claimed the guy collected antique cars. Those were her words, "antique cars." But they were just clunkers.

I had his number. Mr. Fixit.

But we had things in common, Ross and me, which was more than just the same woman. For example, he couldn't fix the TV when it went crazy and we lost the picture. I couldn't fix it either. We had volume, but no picture. If we wanted the news, we had to sit around the screen and listen.

Ross and Myrna met when Myrna was trying to stay sober. She was going to meetings, I'd say, three or four times a week. I had been in and out myself. But when Myrna met Ross, I was out and drinking a fifth a day. Myrna went to the meetings, and then she went over to Mr. Fixit's house to cook for him and clean up. His kids were no help in this regard. Nobody lifted a hand around Mr. Fixit's house, except my wife when she was there.

ALL this happened not too long ago, three years about. It was something in those days.

I left my mother with the man on her sofa and drove around for a while. When I got home, Myrna made me a coffee.

She went out to the kitchen to do it while I waited until I heard her running water. Then I reached under a cushion for the bottle.

I think maybe Myrna really loved the man. But he also had a little something on the side—a twenty-two-year-old named Beverly. Mr. Fixit did okay for a little guy who wore a button-up sweater.

He was in his mid-thirties when he went under. Lost his job and took up the bottle. I used to make fun of him when I had the chance. But I don't make fun of him anymore.

God bless and keep you, Mr. Fixit.

He told Melody he'd worked on the moon shots. He told my daughter he was close friends with the astronauts. He told her he was going to introduce her to the astronauts as soon as they came to town.

It's a modern operation out there, the aerospace place where Mr. Fixit used to work. I've seen it. Cafeteria lines, executive dining rooms, and the like. Mr. Coffees in every office.

Mr. Coffee and Mr. Fixit.

Myrna says he was interested in astrology, auras, I Ching —that business. I don't doubt that this Ross was bright enough and interesting, like most of our ex-friends. I told Myrna I was sure she wouldn't have cared for him if he wasn't.

MY dad died in his sleep, drunk, eight years ago. It was a Friday noon and he was fifty-four. He came home from work at the sawmill, took some sausage out of the freezer for his breakfast, and popped a quart of Four Roses.

My mother was there at the same kitchen table. She was trying to write a letter to her sister in Little Rock. Finally, my dad got up and went to bed. My mother said he never said good night. But it was morning, of course.

"Honey," I said to Myrna the night she came home. "Let's hug awhile and then you fix us a real nice supper."

Myrna said, "Wash your hands."

Gazebo

THAT morning she pours Teacher's over my belly and licks it off. That afternoon she tries to jump out the window.

I go, "Holly, this can't continue. This has got to stop."

We are sitting on the sofa in one of the upstairs suites. There were any number of vacancies to choose from. But we needed a suite, a place to move around in and be able to talk. So we'd locked up the motel office that morning and gone upstairs to a suite.

She goes, "Duane, this is killing me."

We are drinking Teacher's with ice and water. We'd slept awhile between morning and afternoon. Then she was out of bed and threatening to climb out the window in her undergarments. I had to get her in a hold. We were only two floors up. But even so.

"I've had it," she goes. "I can't take it anymore."

She puts her hand to her cheek and closes her eyes. She turns her head back and forth and makes this humming noise.

I could die seeing her like this.

"Take what?" I go, though of course I know.

"I don't have to spell it out for you again," she goes. "I've lost control. I've lost pride. I used to be a proud woman."

She's an attractive woman just past thirty. She is tall and has long black hair and green eyes, the only green-eyed woman I've ever known. In the old days I used to say things about her green eyes, and she'd tell me it was because of them she knew she was meant for something special.

And didn't I know it!

I feel so awful from one thing and the other.

I can hear the telephone ringing downstairs in the office. It has been ringing off and on all day. Even when I was dozing I could hear it. I'd open my eyes and look at the ceiling and listen to it ring and wonder at what was happening to us.

But maybe I should be looking at the floor.

"My heart is broken," she goes. "It's turned to a piece of stone. I'm no good. That's what's as bad as anything, that I'm no good anymore."

"Holly," I go.

WHEN we'd first moved down here and taken over as managers, we thought we were out of the woods. Free rent and free utilities plus three hundred a month. You couldn't beat it with a stick.

Holly took care of the books. She was good with figures, and she did most of the renting of the units. She liked people, and people liked her back. I saw to the grounds, mowed the grass and cut weeds, kept the swimming pool clean, did the small repairs.

Everything was fine for the first year. I was holding down another job nights, and we were getting ahead. We had plans. Then one morning, I don't know. I'd just laid some bathroom tile in one of the units when this little Mexican maid comes in to clean. It was Holly had hired her. I can't really say I'd noticed the little thing before, though we spoke when we saw each other. She called me, I remember, Mister.

Anyway, one thing and the other.

So after that morning I started paying attention. She was a neat little thing with fine white teeth. I used to watch her mouth.

She started calling me by my name.

One morning I was doing a washer for one of the bathroom faucets, and she comes in and turns on the TV as maids are like to do. While they clean, that is. I stopped what I was doing and stepped outside the bathroom. She was surprised to see me. She smiles and says my name.

It was right after she said it that we got down on the bed.

"HOLLY, you're still a proud woman," I go. "You're still number one. Come on, Holly."

She shakes her head.

"Something's died in me," she goes. "It took a long time for it to do it, but it's dead. You've killed something, just like you'd took an axe to it. Everything is dirt now."

She finishes her drink. Then she begins to cry. I make to hug her. But it's no good.

I freshen our drinks and look out the window.

Two cars with out-of-state plates are parked in front of the office, and the drivers are standing at the door, talking. One of them finishes saying something to the other, and looks around at the units and pulls his chin. There's a woman there too, and she has her face up to the glass, hand shielding her eyes, peering inside. She tries the door.

The phone downstairs begins to ring.

"Even a while ago when we were doing it, you were thinking of her," Holly goes. "Duane, this is hurtful."

She takes the drink I give her.

"Holly," I go.

"It's true, Duane," she goes. "Just don't argue with me," she goes.

She walks up and down the room in her underpants and her brassiere, her drink in her hand.

Holly goes, "You've gone outside the marriage. It's trust that you killed."

I get down on my knees and I start to beg. But I am thinking of Juanita. This is awful. I don't know what's going to happen to me or to anyone else in the world.

I go, "Holly, honey, I love you."

In the lot someone leans on a horn, stops, and then leans again.

Holly wipes her eyes. She goes, "Fix me a drink. This one's too watery. Let them blow their stinking horns. I don't care. I'm moving to Nevada."

"Don't move to Nevada," I go. "You're talking crazy," I go.

"I'm not talking crazy," she goes. "Nothing's crazy about Nevada. You can stay here with your cleaning woman. I'm moving to Nevada. Either there or kill myself."

"Holly!" I go.

"Holly *nothing*!" she goes.

She sits on the sofa and draws her knees up to under her chin.

"Fix me another pop, you son of a bitch," she goes. She goes, "Fuck those horn-blowers. Let them do their dirt in the Travelodge. Is that where your cleaning woman cleans now? Fix me another, you son of a bitch!"

She sets her lips and gives me her special look.

DRINKING'S funny. When I look back on it, all of our important decisions have been figured out when we were drinking. Even when we talked about having to cut back on our drinking, we'd be sitting at the kitchen table or out at the picnic table with a six-pack or whiskey. When we made up our minds to move down here and take this job as managers, we sat up a couple of nights drinking while we weighed the pros and the cons.

I pour the last of the Teacher's into our glasses and add cubes and a spill of water.

Holly gets off the sofa and stretches on out across the bed.

She goes, "Did you do it to her in this bed?"

I don't have anything to say. I feel all out of words inside. I give her the glass and sit down in the chair. I drink my drink and think it's not ever going to be the same.

"Duane?" she goes.

"Holly?"

My heart has slowed. I wait.

Holly was my own true love.

THE thing with Juanita was five days a week between the hours of ten and eleven. It was in whatever unit she was in when she was making her cleaning rounds. I'd just walk in where she was working and shut the door behind me.

But mostly it was in 11. It was 11 that was our lucky room.

We were sweet with each other, but swift. It was fine.

I think Holly could maybe have weathered it out. I think the thing she had to do was really give it a try.

Me, I held on to the night job. A monkey could do that work. But things here were going downhill fast. We just didn't have the heart for it anymore.

I stopped cleaning the pool. It filled up with green gick so that the guests wouldn't use it anymore. I didn't fix any more faucets or lay any more tile or do any of the touch-up painting. Well, the truth is we were both hitting it pretty hard. Booze takes a lot of time and effort if you're going to do a good job with it.

Holly wasn't registering the guests right, either. She was charging too much or else not collecting what she should. Sometimes she'd put three people to a room with only one bed in it, or else she'd put a single in where the bed was a king-size. I tell you, there were complaints, and sometimes there were words. Folks would load up and go somewhere else.

The next thing, there's a letter from the management people. Then there's another, certified.

There's telephone calls. There's someone coming down from the city.

But we had stopped caring, and that's a fact. We knew our days were numbered. We had fouled our lives and we were getting ready for a shake-up.

Holly's a smart woman. She knew it first.

THEN that Saturday morning we woke up after a night of rehashing the situation. We opened our eyes and turned in bed to take a good look at each other. We both knew it then. We'd reached the end of something, and the thing was to find out where new to start.

We got up and got dressed, had coffee, and decided on this talk. Without nothing interrupting. No calls. No guests.

That's when I got the Teacher's. We locked up and came upstairs here with ice, glasses, bottles. First off, we watched the color TV and frolicked some and let the phone ring away downstairs. For food, we went out and got cheese crisps from the machine.

There was this funny thing of anything could happen now that we realized everything had.

"WHEN we were just kids before we married?" Holly goes. "When we had big plans and hopes? You remember?" She was sitting on the bed, holding her knees and her drink.

"I remember, Holly."

"You weren't my first, you know. My first was Wyatt. Imagine. Wyatt. And your name's Duane. Wyatt and Duane.

Who knows what I was missing all those years? You were my everything, just like the song."

I go, "You're a wonderful woman, Holly. I know you've had the opportunities."

"But I didn't take them up on it!" she goes. "I couldn't go outside the marriage."

"Holly, please," I go. "No more now, honey. Let's not torture ourselves. What is it we should do?"

"Listen," she goes. "You remember the time we drove out to that old farm place outside of Yakima, out past Terrace Heights? We were just driving around? We were on this little dirt road and it was hot and dusty? We kept going and came to that old house, and you asked if could we have a drink of water? Can you imagine us doing that now? Going up to a house and asking for a drink of water?

"Those old people must be dead now," she goes, "side by side out there in some cemetery. You remember they asked us in for cake? And later on they showed us around? And there was this gazebo there out back? It was out back under some trees? It had a little peaked roof and the paint was gone and there were these weeds growing up over the steps. And the woman said that years before, I mean a real long time ago, men used to come around and play music out there on a Sunday, and the people would sit and listen. I thought we'd be like that too when we got old enough. Dignified. And in a place. And people would come to our door."

I can't say anything just yet. Then I go, "Holly, these things, we'll look back on them too. We'll go, 'Remember the motel with all the crud in the pool?'" I go, "You see what I'm saying, Holly?"

But Holly just sits there on the bed with her glass.

I can see she doesn't know.

I move over to the window and look out from behind the curtain. Someone says something below and rattles the door to the office. I stay there. I pray for a sign from Holly. I pray for Holly to show me.

I hear a car start. Then another. They turn on their lights against the building and, one after the other, they pull away and go out into the traffic.

"Duane," Holly goes.

In this, too, she was right.

I Could See the Smallest Things

I WAS in bed when I heard the gate. I listened carefully. I didn't hear anything else. But I heard that. I tried to wake Cliff. He was passed out. So I got up and went to the window. A big moon was laid over the mountains that went around the city. It was a white moon and covered with scars. Any damn fool could imagine a face there.

There was light enough so that I could see everything in the yard—lawn chairs, the willow tree, clothesline strung between the poles, the petunias, the fences, the gate standing wide open.

But nobody was moving around. There were no scary shadows. Everything lay in moonlight, and I could see the smallest things. The clothespins on the line, for instance.

I put my hands on the glass to block out the moon. I

looked some more. I listened. Then I went back to bed.

But I couldn't get to sleep. I kept turning over. I thought about the gate standing open. It was like a dare.

Cliff's breathing was awful to listen to. His mouth gaped open and his arms hugged his pale chest. He was taking up his side of the bed and most of mine.

I pushed and pushed on him. But he just groaned.

I stayed still awhile longer until I decided it was no use. I got up and got my slippers. I went to the kitchen and made tea and sat with it at the kitchen table. I smoked one of Cliff's unfiltereds.

It was late. I didn't want to look at the time. I drank the tea and smoked another cigarette. After a while I decided I'd go out and fasten up the gate.

So I got my robe.

The moon lighted up everything—houses and trees, poles and power lines, the whole world. I peered around the backyard before I stepped off the porch. A little breeze came along that made me close the robe.

I started for the gate.

THERE was a noise at the fences that separated our place from Sam Lawton's place. I took a sharp look. Sam was leaning with his arms on his fence, there being two fences to lean on. He raised his fist to his mouth and gave a dry cough.

"Evening, Nancy," Sam Lawton said.

I said, "Sam, you scared me." I said, "What are you doing up?" "Did you hear something?" I said. "I heard my gate unlatch."

He said, "I didn't hear anything. Haven't seen anything, either. It might have been the wind."

He was chewing something. He looked at the open gate and shrugged.

His hair was silvery in the moonlight and stood up on his head. I could see his long nose, the lines in his big sad face.

I said, "What are you doing up, Sam?" and moved closer to the fence.

"Want to see something?" he said.

"I'll come around," I said.

I let myself out and went along the walk. It felt funny walking around outside in my nightgown and my robe. I thought to myself that I should try to remember this, walking around outside like this.

Sam was standing over by the side of his house, his pajamas way up high over his tan-and-white shoes. He was holding a flashlight in one hand and a can of something in the other.

SAM and Cliff used to be friends. Then one night they got to drinking. They had words. The next thing, Sam had built a fence and then Cliff built one too.

That was after Sam had lost Millie, gotten married again, and become a father again all in the space of no time at all. Millie had been a good friend to me up until she died. She was only forty-five when she did it. Heart failure. It hit her just as she was coming into their drive. The car kept going and went on through the back of the carport.

"Look at this," Sam said, hitching his pajama trousers and squatting down. He pointed his light at the ground.

I looked and saw some wormy things curled on a patch of dirt.

"Slugs," he said. "I just gave them a dose of this," he said, raising a can of something that looked like Ajax. "They're taking over," he said, and worked whatever it was that he had in his mouth. He turned his head to one side and spit what could have been tobacco. "I have to keep at this to just come close to staying up with them." He turned his light on a jar that was filled with the things. "I put bait out, and then every chance I get I come out here with this stuff. Bastards are all over. A crime what they can do. Look here," he said.

He got up. He took my arm and moved me over to his rosebushes. He showed me the little holes in the leaves.

"Slugs," he said. "Everywhere you look around here at night. I lay out bait and then I come out and get them," he said. "An awful invention, the slug. I save them up in that jar there." He moved his light to under the rosebush.

A plane passed overhead. I imagined the people on it sitting belted in their seats, some of them reading, some of them staring down at the ground.

"Sam," I said, "how's everybody?"

"They're fine," he said, and shrugged.

He chewed on whatever it was he was chewing. "How's Clifford?" he said.

I said, "Same as ever."

Sam said, "Sometimes when I'm out here after the slugs, I'll look over in your direction." He said, "I wish me and Cliff was friends again. Look there now," he said, and drew a sharp breath. "There's one there. See him? Right there where my light is." He had the beam directed onto the dirt under the rosebush. "Watch this," Sam said.

I closed my arms under my breasts and bent over to where he was shining his light. The thing stopped moving and turned its head from side to side. Then Sam was over it with his can of powder, sprinkling the powder down.

"Slimy things," he said.

The slug was twisting this way and that. Then it curled and straightened out.

Sam picked up a toy shovel, and scooped the slug into it, and dumped it out in the jar.

"I quit, you know," Sam said. "Had to. For a while it was getting so I didn't know up from down. We still keep it around the house, but I don't have much to do with it anymore."

I nodded. He looked at me and he kept looking.

"I'd better get back," I said.

"Sure," he said. "I'll continue with what I'm doing and then when I'm finished, I'll head in too."

I said, "Good night, Sam."

He said, "Listen." He stopped chewing. With his tongue, he pushed whatever it was behind his lower lip. "Tell Cliff I said hello."

I said, "I'll tell him you said so, Sam."

Sam ran his hand through his silvery hair as if he was going to make it sit down once and for all, and then he used his hand to wave.

IN the bedroom, I took off the robe, folded it, put it within reach. Without looking at the time, I checked to make sure the stem was out on the clock. Then I got into the bed, pulled the covers up, and closed my eyes.

It was then that I remembered I'd forgotten to latch the gate.

I opened my eyes and lay there. I gave Cliff a little shake. He cleared his throat. He swallowed. Something caught and dribbled in his chest.

I don't know. It made me think of those things that Sam Lawton was dumping powder on.

I thought for a minute of the world outside my house, and then I didn't have any more thoughts except the thought that I had to hurry up and sleep.

SACKS

IT'S October, a damp day. From my hotel window I can see too much of this Midwestern city. I can see lights coming on in some of the buildings, smoke from the tall stacks rising in a thick climb. I wish I didn't have to look.

I want to pass along to you a story my father told me when I stopped over in Sacramento last year. It concerns some events that involved him two years before that time, that time being before he and my mother were divorced.

I'm a book salesman. I represent a well-known organization. We put out textbooks, and the home base is Chicago. My territory is Illinois, parts of Iowa and Wisconsin. I had been attending the Western Book Publishers Association convention in Los Angeles when it occurred to me to visit a few hours with my father. I had not seen him since the divorce, you understand. So I got his address out of my wallet and sent him a wire. The next morning I sent my things on to Chicago and boarded a plane for Sacramento.

IT took me a minute to pick him out. He was standing where everyone else was—behind the gate, that is—white hair, glasses, brown Sta-Prest pants.

"Dad, how are you?" I said.

He said, "Les."

We shook hands and moved toward the terminal.

"How's Mary and the kids?" he said.

"Everyone's fine," I said, which was not the truth.

He opened a white confectionary sack. He said, "I picked up a little something you could maybe take back with you. Not much. Some Almond Roca for Mary, and some jelly-beans for the kids."

"Thanks," I said.

"Don't forget this when you leave," he said.

We moved out of the way as some nuns came running for the boarding area.

"A drink or a cup of coffee?" I said.

"Anything you say," he said. "But I don't have a car," he said.

We located the lounge, got drinks, lit cigarettes.

"Here we are," I said.

"Well, yes," he said.

I shrugged and said, "Yes."

I leaned back in the seat and drew a long breath, inhaling from what I took to be the air of woe that circled his head.

He said, "I guess the Chicago airport would make four of this one."

"More than that," I said.

"Thought it was big," he said.

"When did you start wearing glasses?" I said.

"A while ago," he said.

He took a good swallow, and then he got right down to it.

"I liked to have died over it," he said. He rested his heavy arms on either side of his glass. "You're an educated man, Les. You'll be the one to figure it out."

I turned the ashtray on its edge to read what was on the bottom: HARRAH'S CLUB / RENO AND LAKE TAHOE / GOOD PLACES TO HAVE FUN.

"She was a Stanley Products woman. A little woman, small feet and hands and coal-black hair. She wasn't the most beautiful thing in the world. But she had these nice ways about her. She was thirty and had kids. But she was a decent woman, whatever happened.

"Your mother was always buying from her, a broom, a mop, some kind of pie filling. You know your mother. It was a Saturday, and I was home. Your mother was gone someplace. I don't know where she was. She wasn't working. I was in the front room reading the paper and having a cup of coffee when there was this knock on the door and it was this little woman. Sally Wain. She said she had some things for Mrs. Palmer. 'I'm Mr. Palmer,' I says. 'Mrs. Palmer is not here now,' I says. I ask her just to step in, you know, and I'd pay her for the things. She didn't know whether she should or not. Just stands there holding this little paper sack and the receipt with it.

"'Here, I'll take that,' I says. 'Why don't you come in and sit down a minute till I see if I can find some money.'

"'That's all right,' she says. 'You can owe it. I have lots of people do that. It's all right.' She smiles to let me know it was all right, you see.

"'No, no,' I says. 'I've got it. I'd sooner pay it now. Save you a trip back and save me owing. Come in,' I said, and I hold the screen door open. It wasn't polite to have her standing out there."

He coughed and took one of my cigarettes. From down the bar a woman laughed. I looked at her and then I read from the ashtray again.

"She steps in, and I says. 'Just a minute, please,' and I go into the bedroom to look for my wallet. I look around on the dresser, but I can't find it. I find some change and matches and my comb, but I can't find my wallet. Your mother has gone through that morning cleaning up, you see. So I go back to the front room and says, 'Well, I'll turn up some money yet.'

"'Please, don't bother,' she says.

"'No bother,' I says. 'Have to find my wallet, anyway. Make yourself at home.'

"'Oh, I'm fine,' she says.

"'Look here,' I says. 'You hear about that big holdup back East? I was just reading about it.'

"'I saw it on the TV last night,' she says.

"'They got away clean,' I says.

"'Pretty slick,' she says.

"'The perfect crime,' I says.

"'Not many people get away with it,' she says.

"I didn't know what else to say. We were just standing there looking at each other. So I went on out to the porch and looked for my pants in the hamper, where I figured your mother had put them. I found the wallet in my back pocket and went back to the other room and asked how much I owed.

"It was three or four dollars, and I paid her. Then, I don't know why, I asked her what she'd do with it if she had it, all the money those robbers got away with.

"She laughed and I saw her teeth.

"I don't know what came over me then, Les. Fifty-five years old. Grown kids. I knew better than that. This woman was half my age with little kids in school. She did this Stanley job just the hours they were in school, just to give her something to keep busy. She didn't have to work. They had enough to get by on. Her husband, Larry, he was a driver for Consolidated Freight. Made good money. Teamster, you know."

He stopped and wiped his face.

"Anybody can make a mistake," I said.

He shook his head.

"She had these two boys, Hank and Freddy. About a year apart. She showed me some pictures. Anyway, she laughs when I say that about the money, says she guessed she'd quit selling Stanley Products and move to Dago and buy a house. She said she had relations in Dago."

I lit another cigarette. I looked at my watch. The bartender raised his eyebrows and I raised my glass.

"So she's sitting down on the sofa now and she asks me do I have a cigarette. Said she'd left hers in her other purse, and how she hadn't had a smoke since she left home. Says she hated to buy from a machine when she had a carton at home. I gave her a cigarette and I hold a match for her. But I can tell you, Les, my fingers were shaking."

He stopped and studied the bottles for a minute. The woman who'd done the laughing had her arms locked through the arms of the men on either side of her.

"IT'S fuzzy after that. I remember I asked her if she wanted coffee. Said I'd just made a fresh pot. She said she had to be going. She said maybe she had time for one cup. I went out to the kitchen and waited for the coffee to heat. I tell you, Les, I'll swear before God, I never once stepped out on your mother the whole time we were man and wife. Not once. There were times when I felt like it and had the chance. I tell you, you don't know your mother like I do."

I said, "You don't have to say anything in that direction."

"I took her her coffee, and she's taken off her coat by now. I sit down on the other end of the sofa from her and we get to talking more personal. She says she's got two kids in Roosevelt grade school, and Larry, he was a driver and was sometimes gone for a week or two. Up to Seattle, or down to L.A., or maybe to Phoenix. Always someplace. She says she met Larry when they were going to high school. Said she was proud of the fact she'd gone all the way through. Well, pretty soon she gives a little laugh at something I'd said. It was a thing that could maybe be taken two ways. Then she asks if I'd heard the one about the traveling shoe-salesman who called on the widow woman. We laughed over that one, and then I told her one a little worse. So then she laughs hard at that and smokes another cigarette. One thing's leading to another, is what's happening, don't you see.

"Well, I kissed her then. I put her head back on the sofa and I kissed her, and I can feel her tongue out there rushing to get in my mouth. You see what I'm saying? A man can go along obeying all the rules and then it don't matter a damn anymore. His luck just goes, you know?

"But it was all over in no time at all. And afterwards she says, 'You must think I'm a whore or something,' and then she just goes.

"I was so excited, you know? I fixed up the sofa and turned over the cushions. I folded all the newspapers and even washed the cups we'd used. I cleaned out the coffee pot. All the time what I was thinking about was how I was going to have to face your mother. I was scared.

"Well, that's how it started. Your mother and I went along the same as usual. But I took to seeing that woman regular."

The woman down the bar got off her stool. She took some steps toward the center of the floor and commenced to dance. She tossed her head from side to side and snapped her fingers. The bartender stopped doing drinks. The woman raised her arms above her head and moved in a small circle in the middle of the floor. But then she stopped doing it and the bartender went back to work.

"Did you see that?" my father said.

But I didn't say anything at all.

"SO that's the way it went," he said. "Larry has this schedule, and I'd be over there every time I had the chance. I'd tell your mother I was going here or going there."

He took off his glasses and shut his eyes. "I haven't told this to nobody."

There was nothing to say to that. I looked out at the field and then at my watch.

"Listen," he said. "What time does your plane leave? Can

you take a different plane? Let me buy us another drink, Les. Order us two more. I'll speed it up. I'll be through with this in a minute. *Listen,*" he said.

"She kept his picture in the bedroom by the bed. First it bothered me, seeing his picture there and all. But after a while I got used to it. You see how a man gets used to things?" He shook his head. "Hard to believe. Well, it all come to a bad end. You know that. You know all about that."

"I only know what you tell me," I said.

"I'll tell you, Les. I'll tell you what's the most important thing involved here. You see, there are things. More important things than your mother leaving me. Now, you listen to this. We were in bed one time. It must have been around lunchtime. We were just laying there talking. I was dozing maybe. It's that funny kind of dreaming dozing, you know. But at the same time, I'm telling myself I better remember that pretty soon I got to get up and go. So it's like this when this car pulls into the driveway and somebody gets out and slams the door.

" 'My God,' she screams. 'It's Larry!'

"I must have gone crazy. I seem to remember thinking that if I run out the back door he's going to pin me up against this big fence in the yard and maybe kill me. Sally is making a funny kind of sound. Like she couldn't get her breath. She has her robe on, but it's not closed up, and she's standing in the kitchen shaking her head. All this is happening all at once, you understand. So there I am, almost naked with my clothes in my hand, and Larry is opening the front door. Well, I jump. I just jump right into their picture window, right in there through the glass."

"You got away?" I said. "He didn't come after you?"

My father looked at me as if I were crazy. He stared at his empty glass. I looked at my watch, stretched. I had a small headache behind my eyes.

I said, "I guess I better be getting out there soon." I ran my hand over my chin and straightened my collar. "She still in Redding, that woman?"

"You don't know anything, do you?" my father said. "You don't know anything at all. You don't know anything except how to sell books."

It was almost time to go.

"Ah, God, I'm sorry," he said. "The man went all to pieces, is what. He got down on the floor and cried. She stayed out in the kitchen. She did her crying out there. She got down on her knees and she prayed to God, good and loud so the man would hear."

My father started to say something more. But instead he shook his head. Maybe he wanted me to say something.

But then he said, "No, you got to catch a plane."

I helped him into his coat and we started out, my hand guiding him by the elbow.

"I'll put you in a cab," I said.

He said, "I'll see you off."

"That's all right," I said. "Next time maybe."

We shook hands. That was the last I've seen of him. On the way to Chicago, I remembered how I'd left his sack of gifts on the bar. Just as well. Mary didn't need candy, Almond Roca or anything else.

That was last year. She needs it now even less.

The Bath

SATURDAY afternoon the mother drove to the bakery in the shopping center. After looking through a loose-leaf binder with photographs of cakes taped onto the pages, she ordered chocolate, the child's favorite. The cake she chose was decorated with a spaceship and a launching pad under a sprinkling of white stars. The name SCOTTY would be iced on in green as if it were the name of the spaceship.

The baker listened thoughtfully when the mother told him Scotty would be eight years old. He was an older man, this baker, and he wore a curious apron, a heavy thing with loops that went under his arms and around his back and then crossed in front again where they were tied in a very thick knot. He kept wiping his hands on the front of the apron as he listened to the woman, his wet eyes examining her lips as she studied the samples and talked.

He let her take her time. He was in no hurry.

The mother decided on the spaceship cake, and then she gave the baker her name and her telephone number. The cake would be ready Monday morning, in plenty of time for the party Monday afternoon. This was all the baker was willing to say. No pleasantries, just this small exchange, the barest information, nothing that was not necessary.

MONDAY morning, the boy was walking to school. He was in the company of another boy, the two boys passing a bag of potato chips back and forth between them. The birthday boy was trying to trick the other boy into telling what he was going to give in the way of a present.

At an intersection, without looking, the birthday boy stepped off the curb, and was promptly knocked down by a car. He fell on his side, his head in the gutter, his legs in the road moving as if he were climbing a wall.

The other boy stood holding the potato chips. He was wondering if he should finish the rest or continue on to school.

The birthday boy did not cry. But neither did he wish to talk anymore. He would not answer when the other boy asked what it felt like to be hit by a car. The birthday boy got up and turned back for home, at which time the other boy waved good-bye and headed off for school.

The birthday boy told his mother what had happened. They sat together on the sofa. She held his hands in her lap.

This is what she was doing when the boy pulled his hands away and lay down on his back.

OF course, the birthday party never happened. The birthday boy was in the hospital instead. The mother sat by the bed. She was waiting for the boy to wake up. The father hurried over from his office. He sat next to the mother. So now the both of them waited for the boy to wake up. They waited for hours, and then the father went home to take a bath.

The man drove home from the hospital. He drove the streets faster than he should. It had been a good life till now. There had been work, fatherhood, family. The man had been lucky and happy. But fear made him want a bath.

He pulled into the driveway. He sat in the car trying to make his legs work. The child had been hit by a car and he was in the hospital, but he was going to be all right. The man got out of the car and went up to the door. The dog was barking and the telephone was ringing. It kept ringing while the man unlocked the door and felt the wall for the light switch.

He picked up the receiver. He said, "I just got in the door!"

"There's a cake that wasn't picked up."

This is what the voice on the other end said.

"What are you saying?" the father said.

"The cake," the voice said. "Sixteen dollars."

The husband held the receiver against his ear, trying to understand. He said, "I don't know anything about it."

"Don't hand me that," the voice said.

The husband hung up the telephone. He went into the

kitchen and poured himself some whiskey. He called the hospital.

The child's condition remained the same.

While the water ran into the tub, the man lathered his face and shaved. He was in the tub when he heard the telephone again. He got himself out and hurried through the house, saying, "Stupid, stupid," because he wouldn't be doing this if he'd stayed where he was in the hospital. He picked up the receiver and shouted, "Hello!"

The voice said, "It's ready."

THE father got back to the hospital after midnight. The wife was sitting in the chair by the bed. She looked up at the husband and then she looked back at the child. From an apparatus over the bed hung a bottle with a tube running from the bottle to the child.

"What's this?" the father said.

"Glucose," the mother said.

The husband put his hand to the back of the woman's head.

"He's going to wake up," the man said.

"I know," the woman said.

In a little while the man said, "Go home and let me take over."

She shook her head. "No," she said.

"Really," he said. "Go home for a while. You don't have to worry. He's sleeping, is all."

A nurse pushed open the door. She nodded to them as she went to the bed. She took the left arm out from under the covers and put her fingers on the wrist. She put the arm back under the covers and wrote on the clipboard attached to the bed.

"How is he?" the mother said.

"Stable," the nurse said. Then she said, "Doctor will be in again shortly."

"I was saying maybe she'd want to go home and get a little rest," the man said. "After the doctor comes."

"She could do that," the nurse said.

The woman said, "We'll see what the doctor says." She brought her hand up to her eyes and leaned her head forward.

The nurse said, "Of course."

THE father gazed at his son, the small chest inflating and deflating under the covers. He felt more fear now. He began shaking his head. He talked to himself like this. The child is fine. Instead of sleeping at home, he's doing it here. Sleep is the same wherever you do it.

THE doctor came in. He shook hands with the man. The woman got up from the chair.

"Ann," the doctor said and nodded. The doctor said, "Let's just see how he's doing." He moved to the bed and touched the boy's wrist. He peeled back an eyelid and then the other. He turned back the covers and listened to the heart. He pressed his fingers here and there on the body. He went to the end of the bed and studied the chart. He noted the time, scribbled on the chart, and then he considered the mother and the father.

This doctor was a handsome man. His skin was moist and

tan. He wore a three-piece suit, a vivid tie, and on his shirt were cufflinks.

The mother was talking to herself like this. He has just come from somewhere with an audience. They gave him a special medal.

The doctor said, "Nothing to shout about, but nothing to worry about. He should wake up pretty soon." The doctor looked at the boy again. "We'll know more after the tests are in."

"Oh, no," the mother said.

The doctor said, "Sometimes you see this."

The father said, "You wouldn't call this a coma, then?"

The father waited and looked at the doctor.

"No, I don't want to call it that," the doctor said. "He's sleeping. It's restorative. The body is doing what it has to do."

"It's a coma," the mother said. "A kind of coma."

The doctor said, "I wouldn't call it that."

He took the woman's hands and patted them. He shook hands with the husband.

THE woman put her fingers on the child's forehead and kept them there for a while. "At least he doesn't have a fever," she said. Then she said, "I don't know. Feel his head."

The man put his fingers on the boy's forehead. The man said, "I think he's supposed to feel this way."

The woman stood there awhile longer, working her lip with her teeth. Then she moved to her chair and sat down.

The husband sat in the chair beside her. He wanted to say something else. But there was no saying what it should be. He took her hand and put it in his lap. This made him feel better. It made him feel he was saying something. They sat like that for a while, watching the boy, not talking. From time to time he squeezed her hand until she took it away.

"I've been praying," she said.

"Me too," the father said. "I've been praying too."

A NURSE came back in and checked the flow from the bottle.

A doctor came in and said what his name was. This doctor was wearing loafers.

"We're going to take him downstairs for more pictures," he said. "And we want to do a scan."

"A scan?" the mother said. She stood between this new doctor and the bed.

"It's nothing," he said.

"My God," she said.

Two orderlies came in. They wheeled a thing like a bed. They unhooked the boy from the tube and slid him over onto the thing with wheels.

IT was after sunup when they brought the birthday boy back out. The mother and father followed the orderlies into the elevator and up to the room. Once more the parents took up their places next to the bed.

They waited all day. The boy did not wake up. The doctor came again and examined the boy again and left after saying the same things again. Nurses came in. Doctors came in. A technician came in and took blood.

"I don't understand this," the mother said to the technician.

"Doctor's orders," the technician said.

The mother went to the window and looked out at the parking lot. Cars with their lights on were driving in and out. She stood at the window with her hands on the sill. She was talking to herself like this. We're into something now, something hard.

She was afraid.

She saw a car stop and a woman in a long coat get into it. She made believe she was that woman. She made believe she was driving away from here to someplace else.

THE doctor came in. He looked tanned and healthier than ever. He went to the bed and examined the boy. He said, "His signs are fine. Everything's good."

The mother said, "But he's sleeping."

"Yes," the doctor said.

The husband said, "She's tired. She's starved."

The doctor said, "She should rest. She should eat. Ann," the doctor said.

"Thank you," the husband said.

He shook hands with the doctor and the doctor patted their shoulders and left.

"I SUPPOSE one of us should go home and check on things," the man said. "The dog needs to be fed."

"Call the neighbors," the wife said. "Someone will feed him if you ask them to."

She tried to think who. She closed her eyes and tried to think anything at all. After a time she said, "Maybe I'll do it. Maybe if I'm not here watching, he'll wake up. Maybe it's because I'm watching that he won't."

"That could be it," the husband said.

"I'll go home and take a bath and put on something clean," the woman said.

"I think you should do that," the man said.

She picked up her purse. He helped her into her coat. She moved to the door, and looked back. She looked at the child, and then she looked at the father. The husband nodded and smiled.

SHE went past the nurses' station and down to the end of the corridor, where she turned and saw a little waiting room, a family in there, all sitting in wicker chairs, a man in a khaki shirt, a baseball cap pushed back on his head, a large woman wearing a housedress, slippers, a girl in jeans, hair in dozens of kinky braids, the table littered with flimsy wrappers and styrofoam and coffee sticks and packets of salt and pepper.

"Nelson," the woman said. "Is it about Nelson?"

The woman's eyes widened.

"Tell me now, lady," the woman said. "Is it about Nelson?"

The woman was trying to get up from her chair. But the man had his hand closed over her arm.

"Here, here," the man said.

"I'm sorry," the mother said. "I'm looking for the elevator. My son is in the hospital. I can't find the elevator."

"Elevator is down that way," the man said, and he aimed a finger in the right direction.

"My son was hit by a car," the mother said. "But he's going to be all right. He's in shock now, but it might be some kind of coma too. That's what worries us, the coma part. I'm going out for a little while. Maybe I'll take a bath. But my husband is with him. He's watching. There's a chance everything will change when I'm gone. My name is Ann Weiss."

The man shifted in his chair. He shook his head.

He said, "Our Nelson."

SHE pulled into the driveway. The dog ran out from behind the house. He ran in circles on the grass. She closed her eyes and leaned her head against the wheel. She listened to the ticking of the engine.

She got out of the car and went to the door. She turned on lights and put on water for tea. She opened a can and fed the dog. She sat down on the sofa with her tea.

The telephone rang.

"Yes!" she said. "Hello!" she said.

"Mrs. Weiss," a man's voice said.

"Yes," she said. "This is Mrs. Weiss. Is it about Scotty?" she said.

"Scotty," the voice said. "It is about Scotty," the voice said. "It has to do with Scotty, yes."

Tell the Women We're Going

BILL Jamison had always been best friends with Jerry Roberts. The two grew up in the south area, near the old fairgrounds, went through grade school and junior high together, and then on to Eisenhower, where they took as many of the same teachers as they could manage, wore each other's shirts and sweaters and pegged pants, and dated and banged the same girls—whichever came up as a matter of course.

Summers they took jobs together—swamping peaches, picking cherries, stringing hops, anything they could do that paid a little and where there was no boss to get on your ass. And then they bought a car together. The summer before their senior year, they chipped in and bought a red '54 Plymouth for $325.

They shared it. It worked out fine.

But Jerry got married before the end of the first semester and dropped out of school to work steady at Robby's Mart.

As for Bill, he'd dated the girl too. Carol was her name, and she went just fine with Jerry, and Bill went over there every chance he got. It made him feel older, having married friends. He'd go over there for lunch or for supper, and they'd listen to Elvis or to Bill Haley and the Comets.

But sometimes Carol and Jerry would start making out right with Bill still there, and he'd have to get up and excuse himself and take a walk to Dezorn's Service Station to get some Coke because there was only the one bed in the apartment, a hide-away that came down in the living room. Or sometimes Jerry and Carol would head off to the bathroom, and Bill would have to move to the kitchen and pretend to be interested in the cupboards and the refrigerator and not trying to listen.

So he stopped going over so much; and then June he graduated, took a job at the Darigold plant, and joined the National Guard. In a year he had a milk route of his own and was going steady with Linda. So Bill and Linda would go over to Jerry and Carol's, drink beer, and listen to records.

Carol and Linda got along fine, and Bill was flattered when Carol said that, confidentially, Linda was "a real person."

Jerry liked Linda too. "She's great," Jerry said.

When Bill and Linda got married, Jerry was best man. The reception, of course, was at the Donnelly Hotel, Jerry and Bill cutting up together and linking arms and tossing off glasses of spiked punch. But once, in the middle of all this happiness, Bill looked at Jerry and thought how much older Jerry looked, a lot older than twenty-two. By then Jerry was the happy father of two kids and had moved up to assistant manager at Robby's, and Carol had one in the oven again.

THEY saw each other every Saturday and Sunday, sometimes oftener if it was a holiday. If the weather was good, they'd be over at Jerry's to barbecue hot dogs and turn the kids loose in the wading pool Jerry had got for next to nothing, like a lot of other things he got from the Mart.

Jerry had a nice house. It was up on a hill overlooking the Naches. There were other houses around, but not too close. Jerry was doing all right. When Bill and Linda and Jerry and Carol got together, it was always at Jerry's place because Jerry had the barbecue and the records and too many kids to drag around.

It was a Sunday at Jerry's place the time it happened.

The women were in the kitchen straightening up. Jerry's girls were out in the yard throwing a plastic ball into the wading pool, yelling, and splashing after it.

Jerry and Bill were sitting in the reclining chairs on the patio, drinking beer and just relaxing.

Bill was doing most of the talking—things about people they knew, about Darigold, about the four-door Pontiac Catalina he was thinking of buying.

Jerry was staring at the clothesline, or at the '68 Chevy hardtop that stood in the garage. Bill was thinking how Jerry was getting to be deep, the way he stared all the time and hardly did any talking at all.

Bill moved in his chair and lighted a cigarette.

He said, "Anything wrong, man? I mean, you know."

Jerry finished his beer and then mashed the can. He shrugged.

"You know," he said.

Bill nodded.

Then Jerry said, "How about a little run?"

"Sounds good to me," Bill said. "I'll tell the women we're going."

THEY took the Naches River highway out to Gleed, Jerry driving. The day was sunny and warm, and air blew through the car.

"Where we headed?" Bill said.

"Let's shoot a few balls."

"Fine with me," Bill said. He felt a whole lot better just seeing Jerry brighten up.

"Guy's got to get out," Jerry said. He looked at Bill. "You know what I mean?"

Bill understood. He liked to get out with the guys from the plant for the Friday-night bowling league. He liked to stop off twice a week after work to have a few beers with Jack Broderick. He knew a guy's got to get out.

"Still standing," Jerry said, as they pulled up onto the gravel in front of the Rec Center.

They went inside, Bill holding the door for Jerry, Jerry punching Bill lightly in the stomach as he went on by.

"Hey there!"

It was Riley.

"Hey, how you boys keeping?"

It was Riley coming around from behind the counter,

grinning. He was a heavy man. He had on a short-sleeved Hawaiian shirt that hung outside his jeans. Riley said, "So how you boys been keeping?"

"Ah, dry up and give us a couple of Olys," Jerry said, winking at Bill. "So how you been, Riley?" Jerry said.

Riley said, "So how you boys doing? Where you been keeping yourselves? You boys getting any on the side? Jerry, the last time I seen you, your old lady was six months gone."

Jerry stood a minute and blinked his eyes.

"So how about the Olys?" Bill said.

They took stools near the window. Jerry said, "What kind of place is this, Riley, that it don't have any girls on a Sunday afternoon?"

Riley laughed. He said, "I guess they're all in church praying for it."

They each had five cans of beer and took two hours to play three racks of rotation and two racks of snooker, Riley sitting on a stool and talking and watching them play, Bill always looking at his watch and then looking at Jerry.

Bill said, "So what do you think, Jerry? I mean, what do you think?" Bill said.

Jerry drained his can, mashed it, then stood for a time turning the can in his hand.

BACK on the highway, Jerry opened it up—little jumps of eighty-five and ninety. They'd just passed an old pickup loaded with furniture when they saw the two girls.

"Look at that!" Jerry said, slowing. "I could use some of that."

Jerry drove another mile or so and then pulled off the road. "Let's go back," Jerry said. "Let's try it."

"Jesus," Bill said. "I don't know."

"I could use some," Jerry said.

Bill said, "Yeah, but I don't know."

"For Christ's sake," Jerry said.

Bill glanced at his watch and then looked all around. He said, "You do the talking. I'm rusty."

Jerry hooted as he whipped the car around.

He slowed when he came nearly even with the girls. He pulled the Chevy onto the shoulder across from them. The girls kept on going on their bicycles, but they looked at each other and laughed. The one on the inside was dark-haired, tall, and willowy. The other was light-haired and smaller. They both wore shorts and halters.

"Bitches," Jerry said. He waited for the cars to pass so he could pull a U.

"I'll take the brunette," he said. He said, "The little one's yours."

Bill moved his back against the front seat and touched the bridge of his sunglasses. "They're not going to do anything," Bill said.

"They're going to be on your side," Jerry said.

He pulled across the road and drove back. "Get ready," Jerry said.

"Hi," Bill said as the girls bicycled up. "My name's Bill," Bill said.

"That's nice," the brunette said.

"Where are you going?" Bill said.

The girls didn't answer. The little one laughed. They kept bicycling and Jerry kept driving.

"Oh, come on now. Where you going?" Bill said.

"No place," the little one said.

"Where's no place?" Bill said.

"Wouldn't you like to know," the little one said.

"I told you my name," Bill said. "What's yours? My friend's Jerry," Bill said.

The girls looked at each other and laughed.

A car came up from behind. The driver hit his horn.

"Cram it!" Jerry shouted.

He pulled off a little and let the car go around. Then he pulled back up alongside the girls.

Bill said, "We'll give you a lift. We'll take you where you want. That's a promise. You must be tired riding those bicycles. You look tired. Too much exercise isn't good for a person. Especially for girls."

The girls laughed.

"You see?" Bill said. "Now tell us your names."

"I'm Barbara, she's Sharon," the little one said.

"All right!" Jerry said. "Now find out where they're going."

"Where you girls going?" Bill said. "Barb?"

She laughed. "No place," she said. "Just down the road."

"Where down the road?"

"Do you want me to tell them?" she said to the other girl.

"I don't care," the other girl said. "It doesn't make any difference," she said. "I'm not going to go anyplace with anybody anyway," the one named Sharon said.

"Where you going?" Bill said. "Are you going to Picture Rock?"

The girls laughed.

"That's where they're going," Jerry said.

He fed the Chevy gas and pulled up off onto the shoulder so that the girls had to come by on his side.

"Don't be that way," Jerry said. He said, "Come on." He said, "We're all introduced."

The girls just rode on by.

"I won't bite you!" Jerry shouted.

The brunette glanced back. It seemed to Jerry she was looking at him in the right kind of way. But with a girl you could never be sure.

Jerry gunned it back onto the highway, dirt and pebbles flying from under the tires.

"We'll be seeing you!" Bill called as they went speeding by.

"It's in the bag," Jerry said. "You see the look that cunt gave me?"

"I don't know," Bill said. "Maybe we should cut for home."

"We got it made!" Jerry said.

HE pulled off the road under some trees. The highway forked here at Picture Rock, one road going on to Yakima, the other heading for Naches, Enumclaw, the Chinook Pass, Seattle.

A hundred yards off the road was a high, sloping, black mound of rock, part of a low range of hills, honeycombed with footpaths and small caves, Indian sign-painting here and there on the cave walls. The cliff side of the rock faced the highway and all over it there were things like this: NACHES 67—GLEED WILDCATS—JESUS SAVES—BEAT YAKIMA—REPENT NOW.

They sat in the car, smoking cigarettes. Mosquitoes came in and tried to get at their hands.

"Wish we had a beer now," Jerry said. "I sure could go for a beer," he said.

Bill said, "Me too," and looked at his watch.

WHEN the girls came into view, Jerry and Bill got out of the car. They leaned against the fender in front.

"Remember," Jerry said, starting away from the car, "the dark one's mine. You got the other one."

The girls dropped their bicycles and started up one of the paths. They disappeared around a bend and then reappeared again, a little higher up. They were standing there and looking down.

"What're you guys following us for?" the brunette called down.

Jerry just started up the path.

The girls turned away and went off again at a trot.

Jerry and Bill kept climbing at a walking pace. Bill was smoking a cigarette, stopping every so often to get a good drag. When the path turned, he looked back and caught a glimpse of the car.

"Move it!" Jerry said.

"I'm coming," Bill said.

They kept climbing. But then Bill had to catch his breath. He couldn't see the car now. He couldn't see the highway, either. To his left and all the way down, he could see a strip of the Naches like a strip of aluminum foil.

Jerry said, "You go right and I'll go straight. We'll cut the cockteasers off."

Bill nodded. He was too winded to speak.

He went higher for a while, and then the path began to drop, turning toward the valley. He looked and saw the girls. He saw them crouched behind an outcrop. Maybe they were smiling.

Bill took out a cigarette. But he could not get it lit. Then Jerry showed up. It did not matter after that.

Bill had just wanted to fuck. Or even to see them naked. On the other hand, it was okay with him if it didn't work out.

He never knew what Jerry wanted. But it started and ended with a rock. Jerry used the same rock on both girls, first on the girl called Sharon and then on the one that was supposed to be Bill's.

After the Denim

EDITH Packer had the tape cassette plugged into her ear, and she was smoking one of his cigarettes. The TV played without any volume as she sat on the sofa with her legs tucked under her and turned the pages of a magazine. James Packer came out of the guest room, which was the room he had fixed up as an office, and Edith Packer took the cord from her ear. She put the cigarette in the ashtray and pointed her foot and wiggled her toes in greeting.

He said, "Are we going or not?"

"I'm going," she said.

Edith Packer liked classical music. James Packer did not. He was a retired accountant. But he still did returns for some old clients, and he didn't like to hear music when he did it.

"If we're going, let's go."

He looked at the TV, and then went to turn it off.

"I'm going," she said.

She closed the magazine and got up. She left the room and went to the back.

He followed her to make sure the back door was locked and also that the porch light was on. Then he stood waiting and waiting in the living room.

It was a ten-minute drive to the community center, which meant they were going to miss the first game.

IN the place where James always parked, there was an old van with markings on it, so he had to keep going to the end of the block.

"Lots of cars tonight," Edith said.

He said, "There wouldn't be so many if we'd been on time."

"There'd still be as many. It's just we wouldn't have seen them." She pinched his sleeve, teasing.

He said, "Edith, if we're going to play bingo, we ought to be here on time."

"Hush," Edith Packer said.

He found a parking space and turned into it. He switched off the engine and cut the lights. He said, "I don't know if I feel lucky tonight. I think I felt lucky when I was doing Howard's taxes. But I don't think I feel lucky now. It's not lucky if you have to start out walking half a mile just to play."

"You stick to me," Edith Packer said. "You'll feel lucky."

"I don't feel lucky yet," James said. "Lock your door."

THERE was a cold breeze. He zipped the windbreaker to his neck, and she pulled her coat closed. They could hear the surf breaking on the rocks at the bottom of the cliff behind the building.

She said, "I'll take one of your cigarettes first."

They stopped under the street lamp at the corner. It was a damaged street lamp, and wires had been added to support it. The wires moved in the wind, made shadows on the pavement.

"When are you going to stop?" he said, lighting his cigarette after he'd lighted hers.

"When you stop," she said. "I'll stop when you stop. Just like it was when you stopped drinking. Like that. Like you."

"I can teach you to do needlework," he said.

"One needleworker in the house is enough," she said.

He took her arm and they kept on walking.

When they reached the entrance, she dropped her cigarette and stepped on it. They went up the steps and into the foyer. There was a sofa in the room, a wooden table, folding chairs stacked up. On the walls were hung photographs of fishing boats and naval vessels, one showing a boat that had turned over, a man standing on the keel and waving.

The Packers passed through the foyer, James taking Edith's arm as they entered the corridor.

SOME clubwomen sat to the side of the far doorway signing people in as they entered the assembly hall, where a game was already in progress, the numbers being called by a woman who stood on the stage.

The Packers hurried to their regular table. But a young couple occupied the Packers' usual places. The girl wore denims, and so did the long-haired man with her. She had rings and bracelets and earrings that made her shiny in the milky light. Just as the Packers came up, the girl turned to the fellow with her and poked her finger at a number on his card. Then she pinched his arm. The fellow had his hair pulled back and tied behind his head, and something else the Packers saw—a tiny gold loop through his earlobe.

JAMES guided Edith to another table, turning to look again before sitting down. First he took off his windbreaker and helped Edith with her coat, and then he stared at the couple who had taken their places. The girl was scanning her cards as the numbers were called, leaning over to check the man's cards too—as if, James thought, the fellow did not have sense enough to look after his own numbers.

James picked up the stack of bingo cards that had been set out on the table. He gave half to Edith. "Pick some winners," he said. "Because I'm taking these three on top. It doesn't matter which ones I pick. Edith, I don't feel lucky tonight."

"Don't you pay it any attention," she said. "They're not hurting anybody. They're just young, that's all."

He said, "This is regular Friday night bingo for the people of this community."

She said, "It's a free country."

She handed back the stack of cards. He put them on the

other side of the table. Then they served themselves from the bowl of beans.

JAMES peeled a dollar bill from the roll of bills he kept for bingo nights. He put the dollar next to his cards. One of the clubwomen, a thin woman with bluish hair and a spot on her neck—the Packers knew her only as Alice—would presently come by with a coffee can. She would collect the coins and bills, making change from the can. It was this woman or another woman who paid off the wins.

The woman on the stage called "I–25," and someone in the hall yelled, "Bingo!"

Alice made her way between the tables. She took up the winning card and held it in her hand as the woman on the stage read out the winning numbers.

"It's a bingo," Alice confirmed.

"That bingo, ladies and gentlemen, is worth twelve dollars!" the woman on the stage announced. "Congratulations to the winner!"

THE Packers played another five games to no effect. James came close once on one of his cards. But then five numbers were called in succession, none of them his, the fifth a number that produced a bingo on somebody else's card.

"You almost had it that time," Edith said. "I was watching your card."

"She was teasing me," James said.

He tilted the card and let the beans slide into his hand. He closed his hand and made a fist. He shook the beans in his fist. Something came to him about a boy who'd thrown some beans out a window. The memory reached to him from a long way off, and it made him feel lonely.

"Change cards, maybe," Edith said.

"It isn't my night," James said.

He looked over at the young couple again. They were laughing at something the fellow had said. James could see they weren't paying attention to anyone else in the hall.

ALICE came around collecting money for the next game, and just after the first number had been called, James saw the fellow in the denims put down a bean on a card he hadn't paid for. Another number was called, and James saw the fellow do it again. James was amazed. He could not concentrate on his own cards. He kept looking up to see what the fellow in denim was doing.

"James, look at your cards," Edith said. "You missed N–34. Pay attention."

"That fellow over there who has our place is cheating. I can't believe my eyes," James said.

"How is he cheating?" Edith said.

"He's playing a card that he hasn't paid for," James said. "Somebody ought to report him."

"Not you, dear," Edith said. She spoke slowly and tried to keep her eyes on her cards. She dropped a bean on a number.

"The fellow is cheating," James said.

She extracted a bean from her palm and placed it on a number. "Play your cards," Edith said.

He looked back at his cards. But he knew he might as well write this game off. There was no telling how many numbers he had missed, how far behind he had fallen. He squeezed the beans in his fist.

The woman on the stage called, "G–60."

Someone yelled, "Bingo!"

"Christ," James Packer said.

A TEN-MINUTE break was announced. The game after the break would be a Blackout, one dollar a card, winner takes all, this week's jackpot ninety-eight dollars.

There was whistling and clapping.

James looked at the couple. The fellow was touching the ring in his ear and staring up at the ceiling. The girl had her hand on his leg.

"I have to go to the bathroom," Edith said. "Give me your cigarettes."

James said, "And I'll get us some raisin cookies and coffee."

"I'll go to the bathroom," Edith said.

But James Packer did not go to get cookies and coffee. Instead, he went to stand behind the chair of the fellow in denim.

"I see what you're doing," James said.

The man turned around. "Pardon me?" he said and stared. "What am I doing?"

"You know," James said.

The girl held her cookie in mid-bite.

"A word to the wise," James said.

He walked back to his table. He was trembling.

When Edith came back, she handed him the cigarettes

and sat down, not talking, not being her jovial self.

James looked at her closely. He said, "Edith, has something happened?"

"I'm spotting again," she said.

"Spotting?" he said. But he knew what she meant. "Spotting," he said again, very quietly.

"Oh, dear," Edith Packer said, picking up some cards and sorting through them.

"I think we should go home," he said.

She kept sorting through the cards. "No, let's stay," she said. "It's just the spotting, is all."

He touched her hand.

"We'll stay," she said. "It'll be all right."

"This is the worst bingo night in history," James Packer said.

THEY played the Blackout game, James watching the man in denim. The fellow was still at it, still playing a card he hadn't paid for. From time to time, James checked how Edith was doing. But there was no way of telling. She held her lips pursed together. It could mean anything—resolve, worry, pain. Or maybe she just liked having her lips that way for this particular game.

He had three numbers to go on one card and five numbers on another, and no chance at all on a third card when the girl with the man in denim began shrieking: "Bingo! Bingo! Bingo! I have a bingo!"

The fellow clapped and shouted with her. "She's got a bingo! She's got a bingo, folks! A bingo!"

The fellow in denim kept clapping.

It was the woman on the stage herself who went to the

girl's table to check her card against the master list. She said, "This young woman has a bingo, and that's a ninety-eight-dollar jackpot! Let's give her a round of applause, people! It's a bingo here! A Blackout!"

Edith clapped along with the rest. But James kept his hands on the table.

The fellow in denim hugged the girl when the woman from the stage handed over the cash.

"They'll use it to buy drugs," James said.

THEY stayed for the rest of the games. They stayed until the last game was played. It was a game called the Progressive, the jackpot increasing from week to week if no one bingoed before so many numbers were called.

James put his money down and played his cards with no hope of winning. He waited for the fellow in denim to call "Bingo!"

But no one won, and the jackpot would be carried over to the following week, the prize bigger than ever.

"That's bingo for tonight!" the woman on the stage proclaimed. "Thank you all for coming. God bless you and good night."

The Packers filed out of the assembly hall along with the rest, somehow managing to fall in behind the fellow in denim and his girl. They saw the girl pat her pocket. They saw the girl put her arm around the fellow's waist.

"Let those people get ahead of us," James said into Edith's ear. "I can't stand to look at them."

Edith said nothing in reply. But she hung back a little to give the couple time to move ahead.

Outside, the wind was up. James thought sure he could

hear the surf over the sound of engines starting.

He saw the couple stop at the van. Of course. He should have put two and two together.

"The dumbbell," James Packer said.

EDITH went into the bathroom and shut the door. James took off his windbreaker and put it down on the back of the sofa. He turned on the TV and took up his place and waited.

After a time, Edith came out of the bathroom. James concentrated his attention on the TV. Edith went to the kitchen and ran water. James heard her turn off the faucet. Edith came to the room and said, "I guess I'll have to see Dr. Crawford in the morning. I guess there really is something happening down there."

"The lousy luck," James said.

She stood there shaking her head. She covered her eyes and leaned into him when he came to put his arms around her.

"Edith, dearest Edith," James Packer said.

He felt awkward and terrified. He stood with his arms more or less holding his wife.

She reached for his face and kissed his lips, and then she said good night.

HE went to the refrigerator. He stood in front of the open door and drank tomato juice while he studied everything inside. Cold air blew out at him. He looked at the little packages and the containers of foodstuffs on the shelves, a chicken covered in plastic wrap, the neat, protected exhibits.

He shut the door and spit the last of the juice into the sink. Then he rinsed his mouth and made himself a cup of instant coffee. He carried it into the living room. He sat down in front of the TV and lit a cigarette. He understood that it took only one lunatic and a torch to bring everything to ruin.

He smoked and finished the coffee, and then he turned the TV off. He went to the bedroom door and listened for a time. He felt unworthy to be listening, to be standing.

Why not someone else? Why not those people tonight? Why not all those people who sail through life free as birds? Why not them instead of Edith?

He moved away from the bedroom door. He thought about going for a walk. But the wind was wild now, and he could hear the branches whining in the birch tree behind the house.

He sat in front of the TV again. But he did not turn it on. He smoked and thought of that sauntering, arrogant gait as the two of them moved just ahead. If only they knew. If only someone would tell them. Just once!

He closed his eyes. He would get up early and fix breakfast. He would go with her to see Crawford. If only they had to sit with him in the waiting room! He'd tell them what to expect! He'd set those floozies straight! He'd tell them what was waiting for you after the denim and the earrings, after touching each other and cheating at games.

HE got up and went into the guest room and turned on the lamp over the bed. He glanced at his papers and at his account books and at the adding machine on his desk. He found a pair of pajamas in one of the drawers. He turned down the covers on the bed. Then he walked back through the house, snapping off lights and checking doors. For a while he stood looking out the kitchen window at the tree shaking under the force of the wind.

He left the porch light on and went back to the guest room. He pushed aside his knitting basket, took up his basket of embroidery, and then settled himself in the chair. He raised the lid of the basket and got out the metal hoop. There was fresh white linen stretched across it. Holding the tiny needle to the light, James Packer stabbed at the eye with a length of blue silk thread. Then he set to work—stitch after stitch—making believe he was waving like the man on the keel.

So Much Water So Close to Home

MY husband eats with a good appetite. But I don't think he's really hungry. He chews, arms on the table, and stares at something across the room. He looks at me and looks away. He wipes his mouth on the napkin. He shrugs, and goes on eating.

"What are you staring at me for?" he says. "What is it?" he says and lays down his fork.

"Was I staring?" I say, and shake my head.

The telephone rings.

"Don't answer it," he says.

"It might be your mother," I say.

"Watch and see," he says.

I pick up the receiver and listen. My husband stops eating.

"What did I tell you?" he says when I hang up. He starts to eat again. Then throws his napkin on his plate. He says, "Goddamn it, why can't people mind their own business? Tell me what I did wrong and I'll listen! I wasn't the only man there. We talked it over and we all decided. We couldn't just turn around. We were five miles from the car. I won't have you passing judgment. Do you hear?"

"You know," I say.

He says, "What do I know, Claire? Tell me what I'm supposed to know. I don't know anything except one thing." He gives me what he thinks is a meaningful look. "She was dead," he says. "And I'm as sorry as anyone else. But she was dead."

"That's the point," I say.

He raises his hands. He pushes his chair away from the table. He takes out his cigarettes and goes out to the back with a can of beer. I see him sit in the lawn chair and pick up the newspaper again.

His name is in there on the first page. Along with the names of his friends.

I close my eyes and hold on to the sink. Then I rake my arm across the drainboard and send the dishes to the floor.

He doesn't move. I know he's heard. He lifts his head as if still listening. But he doesn't move otherwise. He doesn't turn around.

HE and Gordon Johnson and Mel Dorn and Vern Williams, they play poker and bowl and fish. They fish every spring and early summer before visiting relatives can get in the way. They are decent men, family men, men who take care of their jobs. They have sons and daughters who go to school with our son, Dean.

Last Friday these family men left for the Naches River. They parked the car in the mountains and hiked to where they wanted to fish. They carried their bedrolls, their food, their playing cards, their whiskey.

They saw the girl before they set up camp. Mel Dorn found her. No clothes on her at all. She was wedged into some branches that stuck out over the water.

He called the others and they came to look. They talked about what to do. One of the men—my Stuart didn't say which—said they should start back at once. The others stirred the sand with their shoes, said they didn't feel inclined that way. They pleaded fatigue, the late hour, the fact that the girl wasn't going anywhere.

In the end they went ahead and set up the camp. They built a fire and drank their whiskey. When the moon came up, they talked about the girl. Someone said they should keep the body from drifting away. They took their flashlights and went back to the river. One of the men—it might have been Stuart—waded in and got her. He took her by the fingers and pulled her into shore. He got some nylon cord and tied it to her wrist and then looped the rest around a tree.

The next morning they cooked breakfast, drank coffee, and drank whiskey, and then split up to fish. That night they cooked fish, cooked potatoes, drank coffee, drank whiskey, then took their cooking things and eating things back down to the river and washed them where the girl was.

They played some cards later on. Maybe they played

until they couldn't see them anymore. Vern Williams went to sleep. But the others told stories. Gordon Johnson said the trout they'd caught were hard because of the terrible coldness of the water.

The next morning they got up late, drank whiskey, fished a little, took down their tents, rolled their sleeping bags, gathered their stuff, and hiked out. They drove until they got to a telephone. It was Stuart who made the call while the others stood around in the sun and listened. He gave the sheriff their names. They had nothing to hide. They weren't ashamed. They said they'd wait until someone could come for better directions and take down their statements.

I WAS asleep when he got home. But I woke up when I heard him in the kitchen. I found him leaning against the refrigerator with a can of beer. He put his heavy arms around me and rubbed his big hands on my back. In bed he put his hands on me again and then waited as if thinking of something else. I turned and opened my legs. Afterwards, I think he stayed awake.

He was up that morning before I could get out of bed. To see if there was something in the paper, I suppose.

The telephone began ringing right after eight.

"Go to hell!" I heard him shout.

The telephone rang right again.

"I have nothing to add to what I already said to the sheriff!"

He slammed the receiver down.

"What is going on?" I said.

It was then that he told me what I just told you.

I SWEEP up the broken dishes and go outside. He is lying on his back on the grass now, the newspaper and can of beer within reach.

"Stuart, could we go for a drive?" I say.

He rolls over and looks at me. "We'll pick up some beer," he says. He gets to his feet and touches me on the hip as he goes past. "Give me a minute," he says.

We drive through town without speaking. He stops at a roadside market for beer. I notice a great stack of papers just inside the door. On the top step a fat woman in a print dress holds out a licorice stick to a little girl. Later on, we cross Everson Creek and turn into the picnic grounds. The creek runs under the bridge and into a large pond a few hundred yards away. I can see the men out there. I can see them out there fishing.

So much water so close to home.

I say, "Why did you have to go miles away?"

"Don't rile me," he says.

We sit on a bench in the sun. He opens us cans of beer. He says, "Relax, Claire."

"They said they were innocent. They said they were crazy."

He says, "Who?" He says, "What are you talking about?"

"The Maddox brothers. They killed a girl named Arlene Hubly where I grew up. They cut off her head and threw her into the Cle Elum River. It happened when I was a girl."

"You're going to get me riled," he says.

I look at the creek. I'm right in it, eyes open, face down, staring at the moss on the bottom, dead.

"I don't know what's wrong with you," he says on the way home. "You're getting me more riled by the minute."

There is nothing I can say to him.

He tries to concentrate on the road. But he keeps looking into the rear-view mirror.

He knows.

STUART believes he is letting me sleep this morning. But I was awake long before the alarm went off. I was thinking, lying on the far side of the bed away from his hairy legs.

He gets Dean off for school, and then he shaves, dresses, and leaves for work. Twice he looks in and clears his throat. But I keep my eyes closed.

In the kitchen I find a note from him. It's signed "Love."

I sit in the breakfast nook and drink coffee and leave a ring on the note. I look at the newspaper and turn it this way and that on the table. Then I skid it close and read what it says. The body has been identified, claimed. But it took some examining it, some putting things into it, some cutting, some weighing, some measuring, some putting things back again and sewing them in.

I sit for a long time holding the newspaper and thinking. Then I call up to get a chair at the hairdresser's.

I SIT under the dryer with a magazine on my lap and let Marnie do my nails.

"I am going to a funeral tomorrow," I say.

"I'm sorry to hear that," Marnie says.

"It was a murder," I say.

"That's the worst kind," Marnie says.

"We weren't all that close," I say. "But you know."

"We'll get you fixed up for it," Marnie says.

That night I make my bed on the sofa, and in the morning I get up first. I put on coffee and fix breakfast while he shaves.

He appears in the kitchen doorway, towel over his bare shoulder, appraising.

"Here's coffee," I say. "Eggs'll be ready in a minute."

I wake Dean, and the three of us eat. Whenever Stuart looks at me, I ask Dean if he wants more milk, more toast, etc.

"I'll call you today," Stuart says as he opens the door.

I say, "I don't think I'll be home today."

"All right," he says. "Sure."

I dress carefully. I try on a hat and look at myself in the mirror. I write out a note for Dean.

> *Honey, Mommy has things to do this afternoon, but will be back later. You stay in or be in the backyard until one of us comes home.*
>
> *Love, Mommy*

I look at the word *Love* and then I underline it. Then I see the word *backyard*. Is it one word or two?

I DRIVE through farm country, through fields of oats and sugar beets and past apple orchards, cattle grazing in pastures. Then everything changes, more like shacks than farmhouses and stands of timber instead of orchards. Then mountains, and on the right, far below, I sometimes see the Naches River.

A green pickup comes up behind me and stays behind me for miles. I keep slowing at the wrong times, hoping he will pass. Then I speed up. But this is at the wrong times, too. I grip the wheel until my fingers hurt.

On a long clear stretch he goes past. But he drives along beside for a bit, a crewcut man in a blue workshirt. We look each other over. Then he waves, toots his horn, and pulls on up ahead.

I slow down and find a place. I pull over and shut off the motor. I can hear the river down below the trees. Then I hear the pickup coming back.

I lock the doors and roll up the windows.

"You all right?" the man says. He raps on the glass. "You okay?" He leans his arms on the door and brings his face to the window.

I stare at him. I can't think what else to do.

"Is everything all right in there? How come you're all locked up?"

I shake my head.

"Roll down your window." He shakes his head and looks at the highway and then back at me. "Roll it down now."

"Please," I say, "I have to go."

"Open the door," he says as if he isn't listening. "You're going to choke in there."

He looks at my breasts, my legs. I can tell that's what he's doing.

"Hey, sugar," he says. "I'm just here to help is all."

THE casket is closed and covered with floral sprays. The organ starts up the minute I take a seat. People are coming in and finding chairs. There's a boy in flared pants and a yellow short-sleeved shirt. A door opens and the family comes in in a group and moves over to a curtained place off to one side. Chairs creak as everybody gets settled. Directly, a nice blond man in a nice dark suit stands and asks us to bow our heads. He says a prayer for us, the living, and when he finishes, he says a prayer for the soul of the departed.

Along with the others I go past the casket. Then I move out onto the front steps and into the afternoon light. There's a woman who limps as she goes down the stairs ahead of me. On the sidewalk she looks around. "Well, they got him," she says. "If that's any consolation. They arrested him this morning. I heard it on the radio before I come. A boy right here in town."

We move a few steps down the hot sidewalk. People are starting cars. I put out my hand and hold on to a parking meter. Polished hoods and polished fenders. My head swims.

I say, "They have friends, these killers. You can't tell."

"I have known that child since she was a little girl," the woman says. "She used to come over and I'd bake cookies for her and let her eat them in front of the TV."

BACK home, Stuart sits at the table with a drink of whiskey in front of him. For a crazy instant I think something's happened to Dean.

"Where is he?" I say. "Where is Dean?"

"Outside," my husband says.

He drains his glass and stands up. He says, "I think I know what you need."

He reaches an arm around my waist and with his other

hand he begins to unbutton my jacket and then he goes on to the buttons of my blouse.

"First things first," he says.

He says something else. But I don't need to listen. I can't hear a thing with so much water going.

"That's right," I say, finishing the buttons myself. "Before Dean comes. Hurry."

The Third Thing That Killed My Father Off

I'LL tell you what did my father in. The third thing was Dummy, that Dummy died. The first thing was Pearl Harbor. And the second thing was moving to my grandfather's farm near Wenatchee. That's where my father finished out his days, except they were probably finished before that.

My father blamed Dummy's death on Dummy's wife. Then he blamed it on the fish. And finally he blamed himself—because he was the one that showed Dummy the ad in the back of *Field and Stream* for live black bass shipped anywhere in the U.S.

It was after he got the fish that Dummy started acting peculiar. The fish changed Dummy's whole personality. That's what my father said.

I NEVER knew Dummy's real name. If anyone did, I never heard it. Dummy it was then, and it's Dummy I remember him by now. He was a little wrinkled man, bald-headed, short but very powerful in the arms and legs. If he grinned, which was seldom, his lips folded back over brown, broken teeth. It gave him a crafty expression. His watery eyes stayed fastened on your mouth when you were talking—and if you weren't, they'd go to someplace queer on your body.

I don't think he was really deaf. At least not as deaf as he made out. But he sure couldn't talk. That was for certain.

Deaf or no, Dummy'd been on as a common laborer out at the sawmill since the 1920s. This was the Cascade Lumber Company in Yakima, Washington. The years I knew him, Dummy was working as a cleanup man. And all those years I never saw him with anything different on. Meaning a felt hat, a khaki workshirt, a denim jacket over a pair of coveralls. In his top pockets he carried rolls of toilet paper, as one of his jobs was to clean and supply the toilets. It kept him busy, seeing as how the men on nights used to walk off after their tours with a roll or two in their lunchboxes.

Dummy carried a flashlight, even though he worked days. He also carried wrenches, pliers, screwdrivers, friction tape, all the same things the millwrights carried. Well, it made them kid Dummy, the way he was, always carrying everything. Carl Lowe, Ted Slade, Johnny Wait, they were the worst kidders of the ones that kidded Dummy. But Dummy took it all in stride. I think he'd gotten used to it.

My father never kidded Dummy. Not to my knowledge, anyway. Dad was a big, heavy-shouldered man with a crew-haircut, double chin, and a belly of real size. Dummy was always staring at that belly. He'd come to the filing room where my father worked, and he'd sit on a stool and watch my dad's belly while he used the big emery wheels on the saws.

DUMMY had a house as good as anyone's.

It was a tarpaper-covered affair near the river, five or six miles from town. Half a mile behind the house, at the end of a pasture, there lay a big gravel pit that the state had dug when they were paving the roads around there. Three good-sized holes had been scooped out, and over the years they'd filled with water. By and by, the three ponds came together to make one.

It was deep. It had a darkish look to it.

Dummy had a wife as well as a house. She was a woman years younger and said to go around with Mexicans. Father said it was busybodies that said that, men like Lowe and Wait and Slade.

She was a small stout woman with glittery little eyes. The first time I saw her, I saw those eyes. It was when I was with Pete Jensen and we were on our bicycles and we stopped at Dummy's to get a glass of water.

When she opened the door, I told her I was Del Fraser's son. I said, "He works with—" And then I realized. "You know, your husband. We were on our bicycles and thought we could get a drink."

"Wait here," she said.

She came back with a little tin cup of water in each hand. I downed mine in a single gulp.

But she didn't offer us more. She watched us without

saying anything. When we started to get on our bicycles, she came over to the edge of the porch.

"You little fellas had a car now, I might catch a ride with you."

She grinned. Her teeth looked too big for her mouth.

"Let's go," Pete said, and we went.

THERE weren't many places you could fish for bass in our part of the state. There was rainbow mostly, a few brook and Dolly Varden in some of the high mountain streams, and silvers in Blue Lake and Lake Rimrock. That was mostly it, except for the runs of steelhead and salmon in some of the freshwater rivers in late fall. But if you were a fisherman, it was enough to keep you busy. No one fished for bass. A lot of people I knew had never seen a bass except for pictures. But my father had seen plenty of them when he was growing up in Arkansas and Georgia, and he had high hopes to do with Dummy's bass, Dummy being a friend.

The day the fish arrived, I'd gone swimming at the city pool. I remember coming home and going out again to get them since Dad was going to give Dummy a hand—three tanks Parcel Post from Baton Rouge, Louisiana.

We went in Dummy's pickup, Dad and Dummy and me.

These tanks turned out to be barrels, really, the three of them crated in pine lath. They were standing in the shade out back of the train depot, and it took my dad and Dummy both to lift each crate into the truck.

Dummy drove very carefully through town and just as carefully all the way to his house. He went right through his yard without stopping. He went on down to within feet of the pond. By that time it was nearly dark, so he kept his headlights on and took out a hammer and a tire iron from under the seat, and then the two of them lugged the crates up close to the water and started tearing open the first one.

The barrel inside was wrapped in burlap, and there were these nickel-sized holes in the lid. They raised it off and Dummy aimed his flashlight in.

It looked like a million bass fingerlings were finning inside. It was the strangest sight, all those live things busy in there, like a little ocean that had come on the train.

Dummy scooted the barrel to the edge of the water and poured it out. He took his flashlight and shined it into the pond. But there was nothing to be seen anymore. You could hear the frogs going, but you could hear them going anytime it newly got dark.

"Let me get the other crates," my father said, and he reached over as if to take the hammer from Dummy's coveralls. But Dummy pulled back and shook his head.

He undid the other two crates himself, leaving dark drops of blood on the lath where he ripped his hand doing it.

FROM that night on, Dummy was different.

Dummy wouldn't let anyone come around now anymore. He put up fencing all around the pasture, and then he fenced off the pond with electrical barbed wire. They said it cost him all his savings for that fence.

Of course, my father wouldn't have anything to do with Dummy after that. Not since Dummy ran him off. Not from fishing, mind you, because the bass were just babies still. But even from trying to get a look.

One evening two years after, when Dad was working late and I took him his food and a jar of iced tea, I found him standing talking with Syd Glover, the millwright. Just as I came in, I heard Dad saying, "You'd reckon the fool was married to them fish, the way he acts."

"From what I hear," Syd said, "he'd do better to put that fence round his house."

My father saw me then, and I saw him signal Syd Glover with his eyes.

But a month later my dad finally made Dummy do it. What he did was, he told Dummy how you had to thin out the weak ones on account of keeping things fit for the rest of them. Dummy stood there pulling at his ear and staring at the floor. Dad said, Yeah, he'd be down to do it tomorrow because it had to be done. Dummy never said yes, actually. He just never said no, is all. All he did was pull on his ear some more.

WHEN Dad got home that day, I was ready and waiting. I had his old bass plugs out and was testing the treble hooks with my finger.

"You set?" he called to me, jumping out of the car. "I'll go to the toilet, you put the stuff in. You can drive us out there if you want."

I'd stowed everything in the back seat and was trying out the wheel when he came back out wearing his fishing hat and eating a wedge of cake with both hands.

Mother was standing in the door watching. She was a fair-skinned woman, her blonde hair pulled back in a tight bun and fastened down with a rhinestone clip. I wonder if she ever went around back in those happy days, or what she ever really did.

I let out the handbrake. Mother watched until I'd shifted

gears, and then, still unsmiling, she went back inside.

It was a fine afternoon. We had all the windows down to let the air in. We crossed the Moxee Bridge and swung west onto Slater Road. Alfalfa fields stood off to either side, and farther on it was cornfields.

Dad had his hand out the window. He was letting the wind carry it back. He was restless, I could see.

It wasn't long before we pulled up at Dummy's. He came out of the house wearing his hat. His wife was looking out the window.

"You got your frying pan ready?" Dad hollered out to Dummy, but Dummy just stood there eyeing the car. "Hey, Dummy!" Dad yelled. "Hey, Dummy, where's your pole, Dummy?"

Dummy jerked his head back and forth. He moved his weight from one leg to the other and looked at the ground and then at us. His tongue rested on his lower lip, and he began working his foot into the dirt.

I shouldered the creel. I handed Dad his pole and picked up my own.

"We set to go?" Dad said. "Hey, Dummy, we set to go?"

Dummy took off his hat and, with the same hand, he wiped his wrist over his head. He turned abruptly, and we followed him across the spongy pasture. Every twenty feet or so a snipe sprang up from the clumps of grass at the edge of the old furrows.

At the end of the pasture, the ground sloped gently and became dry and rocky, nettle bushes and scrub oaks scattered here and there. We cut to the right, following an old set of car tracks, going through a field of milkweed that came up to our waists, the dry pods at the tops of the stalks rattling angrily as we pushed through. Presently, I saw the sheen of water over Dummy's shoulder, and I heard Dad shout, "Oh, Lord, look at that!"

But Dummy slowed down and kept bringing his hand up and moving his hat back and forth over his head, and then he just stopped flat.

Dad said, "Well, what do you think, Dummy? One place good as another? Where do you say we should come onto it?"

Dummy wet his lower lip.

"What's the matter with you, Dummy?" Dad said. "This your pond, ain't it?"

Dummy looked down and picked an ant off his coveralls.

"Well, hell," Dad said, letting out his breath. He took out his watch. "If it's still all right with you, we'll get to it before it gets too dark."

Dummy stuck his hands in his pockets and turned back to the pond. He started walking again. We trailed along behind. We could see the whole pond now, the water dimpled with rising fish. Every so often a bass would leap clear and come down in a splash.

"Great God," I heard my father say.

WE came up to the pond at an open place, a gravel beach kind of.

Dad motioned to me and dropped into a crouch. I dropped too. He was peering into the water in front of us, and when I looked, I saw what had taken him so.

"Honest to God," he whispered.

A school of bass was cruising, twenty, thirty, not one of them under two pounds. They veered off, and then they shifted and came back, so densely spaced they looked like they were bumping up against each other. I could see their big, heavy-lidded eyes watching us as they went by. They flashed away again, and again they came back.

They were asking for it. It didn't make any difference if we stayed squatted or stood up. The fish just didn't think a thing about us. I tell you, it was a sight to behold.

We sat there for quite a while, watching that school of bass go so innocently about their business, Dummy the whole time pulling at his fingers and looking around as if he expected someone to show up. All over the pond the bass were coming up to nuzzle the water, or jumping clear and falling back, or coming up to the surface to swim along with their dorsals sticking out.

DAD signaled, and we got up to cast. I tell you, I was shaky with excitement. I could hardly get the plug loose from the cork handle of my pole. It was while I was trying to get the hooks out that I felt Dummy seize my shoulder with his big fingers. I looked, and in answer Dummy worked his chin in Dad's direction. What he wanted was clear enough, no more than one pole.

Dad took off his hat and then put it back on and then he moved over to where I stood.

"You go on, Jack," he said. "That's all right, son—you do it now."

I looked at Dummy just before I laid out my cast. His face had gone rigid, and there was a thin line of drool on his chin.

"Come back stout on the sucker when he strikes," Dad said. "Sons of bitches got mouths hard as doorknobs."

I flipped off the drag lever and threw back my arm. I sent her out a good forty feet. The water was boiling even before I had time to take up the slack.

"Hit him!" Dad yelled. "Hit the son of a bitch! Hit him good!"

I came back hard, twice. I had him, all right. The rod bowed over and jerked back and forth. Dad kept yelling what to do.

"Let him go, let him go! Let him run! Give him more line! Now wind in! Wind in! No, let him run! Woo-ee! Will you look at that!"

The bass danced around the pond. Every time it came up out of the water, it shook its head so hard you could hear the plug rattle. And then he'd take off again. But by and by I wore him out and had him in up close. He looked enormous, six or seven pounds maybe. He lay on his side, whipped, mouth open, gills working. My knees felt so weak I could hardly stand. But I held the rod up, the line tight.

Dad waded out over his shoes. But when he reached for the fish, Dummy started sputtering, shaking his head, waving his arms.

"Now what the hell's the matter with you, Dummy? The boy's got hold of the biggest bass I ever seen, and he ain't going to throw him back, by God!"

Dummy kept carrying on and gesturing toward the pond.

"I ain't about to let this boy's fish go. You hear me, Dummy? You got another think coming if you think I'm going to do that."

Dummy reached for my line. Meanwhile, the bass had gained some strength back. He turned himself over and started swimming again. I yelled and then I lost my head and slammed down the brake on the reel and started winding. The bass made a last, furious run.

That was that. The line broke. I almost fell over on my back.

"Come on, Jack," Dad said, and I saw him grabbing up his pole. "Come on, goddamn the fool, before I knock the man down."

THAT February the river flooded.

It had snowed pretty heavy the first weeks of December, and turned real cold before Christmas. The ground froze. The snow stayed where it was. But toward the end of January, the Chinook wind struck. I woke up one morning to hear the house getting buffeted and the steady drizzle of water running off the roof.

It blew for five days, and on the third day the river began to rise.

"She's up to fifteen feet," my father said one evening, looking over his newspaper. "Which is three feet over what you need to flood. Old Dummy going to lose his darlings."

I wanted to go down to the Moxee Bridge to see how high the water was running. But my dad wouldn't let me. He said a flood was nothing to see.

Two days later the river crested, and after that the water began to subside.

Orin Marshall and Danny Owens and I bicycled out to Dummy's one morning a week after. We parked our bicycles and walked across the pasture that bordered Dummy's property.

It was a wet, blustery day, the clouds dark and broken,

moving fast across the sky. The ground was soppy wet and we kept coming to puddles in the thick grass. Danny was just learning how to cuss, and he filled the air with the best he had every time he stepped in over his shoes. We could see the swollen river at the end of the pasture. The water was still high and out of its channel, surging around the trunks of trees and eating away at the edge of the land. Out toward the middle, the current moved heavy and swift, and now and then a bush floated by, or a tree with its branches sticking up.

We came to Dummy's fence and found a cow wedged in up against the wire. She was bloated and her skin was shiny-looking and gray. It was the first dead thing of any size I'd ever seen. I remember Orin took a stick and touched the open eyes.

We moved on down the fence, toward the river. We were afraid to go near the wire because we thought it might still have electricity in it. But at the edge of what looked like a deep canal, the fence came to an end. The ground had simply dropped into the water here, and the fence along with it.

We crossed over and followed the new channel that cut directly into Dummy's land and headed straight for his pond, going into it lengthwise and forcing an outlet for itself at the other end, then twisting off until it joined up with the river farther on.

You didn't doubt that most of Dummy's fish had been carried off. But those that hadn't been were free to come and go.

Then I caught sight of Dummy. It scared me, seeing him.

I motioned to the other fellows, and we all got down.

Dummy was standing at the far side of the pond near where the water was rushing out. He was just standing there, the saddest man I ever saw.

"I SURE do feel sorry for old Dummy, though," my father said at supper a few weeks after. "Mind, the poor devil brought it on himself. But you can't help but be troubled for him."

Dad went on to say George Laycock saw Dummy's wife sitting in the Sportsman's Club with a big Mexican fellow.

"And that ain't the half of it—"

Mother looked up at him sharply and then at me. But I just went on eating like I hadn't heard a thing.

Dad said, "Damn it to hell, Bea, the boy's old enough!"

He'd changed a lot, Dummy had. He was never around any of the men anymore, not if he could help it. No one felt like joking with him either, not since he'd chased Carl Lowe with a two-by-four stud after Carl tipped Dummy's hat off. But the worst of it was that Dummy was missing from work a day or two a week on the average now, and there was some talk of his being laid off.

"The man's going off the deep end," Dad said. "Clear crazy if he don't watch out."

Then on a Sunday afternoon just before my birthday, Dad and I were cleaning the garage. It was a warm, drifty day. You could see the dust hanging in the air. Mother came to the back door and said, "Del, it's for you. I think it's Vern."

I followed Dad in to wash up. When he was through

talking, he put the phone down and turned to us.

"It's Dummy," he said. "Did in his wife with a hammer and drowned himself. Vern just heard it in town."

WHEN we got out there, cars were parked all around. The gate to the pasture stood open, and I could see tire marks that led on to the pond.

The screen door was propped ajar with a box, and there was this lean, pock-faced man in slacks and sports shirt and wearing a shoulder holster. He watched Dad and me get out of the car.

"I was his friend," Dad said to the man.

The man shook his head. "Don't care who you are. Clear off unless you got business here."

"Did they find him?" Dad said.

"They're dragging," the man said, and adjusted the fit of his gun.

"All right if we walk down? I knew him pretty well."

The man said, "Take your chances. They chase you off, don't say you wasn't warned."

We went on across the pasture, taking pretty much the same route we had the day we tried fishing. There were motorboats going on the pond, dirty fluffs of exhaust hanging over it. You could see where the high water had cut away the ground and carried off trees and rocks. The two boats had uniformed men in them, and they were going back and forth, one man steering and the other man handling the rope and hooks.

An ambulance waited on the gravel beach where we'd set ourselves to cast for Dummy's bass. Two men in white lounged against the back, smoking cigarettes.

One of the motorboats cut off. We all looked up. The man in back stood up and started heaving on his rope. After a time, an arm came out of the water. It looked like the hooks had gotten Dummy in the side. The arm went back down and then it came out again, along with a bundle of something.

It's not him, I thought. It's something else that has been in there for years.

The man in the front of the boat moved to the back, and together the two men hauled the dripping thing over the side.

I looked at Dad. His face was funny the way it was set.

"Women," he said. He said, "That's what the wrong kind of woman can do to you, Jack."

BUT I don't think Dad really believed it. I think he just didn't know who to blame or what to say.

It seemed to me everything took a bad turn for my father after that. Just like Dummy, he wasn't the same man anymore. That arm coming up and going back down in the water, it was like so long to good times and hello to bad. Because it was nothing but that all the years after Dummy drowned himself in that dark water.

Is that what happens when a friend dies? Bad luck for the pals he left behind?

But as I said, Pearl Harbor and having to move back to his dad's place didn't do my dad one bit of good, either.

A Serious Talk

VERA'S car was there, no others, and Burt gave thanks for that. He pulled into the drive and stopped beside the pie he'd dropped the night before. It was still there, the aluminum pan upside down, a halo of pumpkin filling on the pavement. It was the day after Christmas.

He'd come on Christmas day to visit his wife and children. Vera had warned him beforehand. She'd told him the score. She'd said he had to be out by six o'clock because her friend and his children were coming for dinner.

They had sat in the living room and solemnly opened the presents Burt had brought over. They had opened his packages while other packages wrapped in festive paper lay piled under the tree waiting for after six o'clock.

He had watched the children open their gifts, waited while Vera undid the ribbon on hers. He saw her slip off the paper, lift the lid, take out the cashmere sweater.

"It's nice," she said. "Thank you, Burt."

"Try it on," his daughter said.

"Put it on," his son said.

Burt looked at his son, grateful for his backing him up.

She did try it on. Vera went into the bedroom and came out with it on.

"It's nice," she said.

"It's nice on *you*," Burt said, and felt a welling in his chest.

He opened his gifts. From Vera, a gift certificate at Sondheim's men's store. From his daughter, a matching comb and brush. From his son, a ballpoint pen.

VERA served sodas, and they did a little talking. But mostly they looked at the tree. Then his daughter got up and began setting the dining-room table, and his son went off to his room.

But Burt liked it where he was. He liked it in front of the fireplace, a glass in his hand, his house, his home.

Then Vera went into the kitchen.

From time to time his daughter walked into the dining room with something for the table. Burt watched her. He watched her fold the linen napkins into the wine glasses. He watched her put a slender vase in the middle of the table. He watched her lower a flower into the vase, doing it ever so carefully.

A small wax and sawdust log burned on the grate. A carton of five more sat ready on the hearth. He got up from the sofa and put them all in the fireplace. He watched until they flamed. Then he finished his soda and made for the patio door. On the way, he saw the pies lined up on the sideboard. He stacked them in his arms, all six, one for every ten times she had ever betrayed him.

In the driveway in the dark, he'd let one fall as he fumbled with the door.

THE front door was permanently locked since the night his key had broken off inside it. He went around to the back. There was a wreath on the patio door. He rapped on the glass. Vera was in her bathrobe. She looked out at him and frowned. She opened the door a little.

Burt said, "I want to apologize to you for last night. I want to apologize to the kids, too."

Vera said, "They're not here."

She stood in the doorway and he stood on the patio next to the philodendron plant. He pulled at some lint on his sleeve.

She said, "I can't take any more. You tried to burn the house down."

"I did not."

"You did. Everybody here was a witness."

He said, "Can I come in and talk about it?"

She drew the robe together at her throat and moved back inside.

She said, "I have to go somewhere in an hour."

He looked around. The tree blinked on and off. There was a pile of colored tissue paper and shiny boxes at one end of the sofa. A turkey carcass sat on a platter in the center of the dining-room table, the leathery remains in a bed of parsley as if in a horrible nest. A cone of ash filled the fireplace. There were some empty Shasta cola cans in there too. A trail of smoke stains rose up the bricks to the mantel, where the wood that stopped them was scorched black.

He turned around and went back to the kitchen.

He said, “What time did your friend leave last night?”

She said, “If you’re going to start that, you can go right now.”

He pulled a chair out and sat down at the kitchen table in front of the big ashtray. He closed his eyes and opened them. He moved the curtain aside and looked out at the backyard. He saw a bicycle without a front wheel standing upside down. He saw weeds growing along the redwood fence.

She ran water into a saucepan. “Do you remember Thanksgiving?” she said. “I said then that was the last holiday you were going to wreck for us. Eating bacon and eggs instead of turkey at ten o’clock at night.”

“I know it,” he said. “I said I’m sorry.”

“Sorry isn’t good enough.”

The pilot light was out again. She was at the stove trying to get the gas going under the pan of water.

“Don’t burn yourself,” he said. “Don’t catch yourself on fire.”

He considered her robe catching fire, him jumping up from the table, throwing her down onto the floor and rolling her over and over into the living room, where he would cover her with his body. Or should he run to the bedroom for a blanket?

“Vera?”

She looked at him.

"Do you have anything to drink? I could use a drink this morning."

"There's some vodka in the freezer."

"When did you start keeping vodka in the freezer?"

"Don't ask."

"Okay," he said, "I won't ask."

He got out the vodka and poured some into a cup he found on the counter.

She said, "Are you just going to drink it like that, out of a cup?" She said, "Jesus, Burt. What'd you want to talk about, anyway? I told you I have someplace to go. I have a flute lesson at one o'clock."

"Are you still taking flute?"

"I just said so. What is it? Tell me what's on your mind, and then I have to get ready."

"I wanted to say I was sorry."

She said, "You said that."

He said, "If you have any juice, I'll mix it with this vodka."

She opened the refrigerator and moved things around.

"There's cranapple juice," she said.

"That's fine," he said.

"I'm going to the bathroom," she said.

He drank the cup of cranapple juice and vodka. He lit a cigarette and tossed the match into the big ashtray that always sat on the kitchen table. He studied the butts in it. Some of them were Vera's brand, and some of them weren't. Some even were lavender-colored. He got up and dumped it all under the sink.

The ashtray was not really an ashtray. It was a big dish of stoneware they'd bought from a bearded potter on the mall in Santa Clara. He rinsed it out and dried it. He put it back on the table. And then he ground out his cigarette in it.

THE water on the stove began to bubble just as the phone began to ring.

He heard her open the bathroom door and call to him through the living room. "Answer that! I'm about to get into the shower."

The kitchen phone was on the counter in a corner behind the roasting pan. He moved the roasting pan and picked up the receiver.

"Is Charlie there?" the voice said.

"No," Burt said.

"Okay," the voice said.

While he was seeing to the coffee, the phone rang again.

"Charlie?"

"Not here," Burt said.

This time he left the receiver off the hook.

VERA came back into the kitchen wearing jeans and a sweater and brushing her hair.

He spooned the instant into the cups of hot water and then spilled some vodka into his. He carried the cups over to the table.

She picked up the receiver, listened. She said, "What's this? Who was on the phone?"

"Nobody," he said. "Who smokes colored cigarettes?"

"I do."

"I didn't know you did that."

"Well, I do."

She sat across from him and drank her coffee. They smoked and used the ashtray.

There were things he wanted to say, grieving things, consoling things, things like that.

"I'm smoking three packs a day," Vera said. "I mean, if you really want to know what goes on around here."

"God almighty," Burt said.

Vera nodded.

"I didn't come over here to hear that," he said.

"What did you come over here to hear, then? You want to hear the house burned down?"

"Vera," he said. "It's Christmas. That's why I came."

"It's the day after Christmas," she said. "Christmas has come and gone," she said. "I don't ever want to see another one."

"What about me?" he said. "You think I look forward to holidays?"

THE phone rang again. Burt picked it up.

"It's someone wanting Charlie," he said.

"What?"

"Charlie," Burt said.

Vera took the phone. She kept her back to him as she talked. Then she turned to him and said, "I'll take this call in the bedroom. So would you please hang up after I've picked it up in there? I can tell, so hang it up when I say."

He took the receiver. She left the kitchen. He held the receiver to his ear and listened. He heard nothing. Then he heard a man clear his throat. Then he heard Vera pick up the other phone. She shouted, "Okay, Burt! I have it now, Burt!"

He put down the receiver and stood looking at it. He opened the silverware drawer and pushed things around inside. He opened another drawer. He looked in the sink. He went into the dining room and got the carving knife. He held it under hot water until the grease broke and ran off. He wiped the blade on his sleeve. He moved to the phone, doubled the cord, and sawed through without any trouble at all. He examined the ends of the cord. Then he shoved the phone back into its corner behind the roasting pan.

SHE came in. She said, "The phone went dead. Did you do anything to the telephone?" She looked at the phone and then picked it up from the counter.

"Son of a bitch!" she screamed. She screamed, "Out, out, where you belong!" She was shaking the phone at him. "That's it! I'm going to get a restraining order, that's what I'm going to get!"

The phone made a *ding* when she banged it down on the counter.

"I'm going next door to call the police if you don't get out of here now!"

He picked up the ashtray. He held it by its edge. He posed with it like a man preparing to hurl the discus.

"Please," she said. "That's our ashtray."

He left through the patio door. He was not certain, but he thought he had proved something. He hoped he had made something clear. The thing was, they had to have a serious talk soon. There were things that needed talking about, important things that had to be discussed. They'd talk again. Maybe after the holidays were over and things got back to normal. He'd tell her the goddamn ashtray was a goddamn dish, for example.

He stepped around the pie in the driveway and got back into his car. He started the car and put it into reverse. It was hard managing until he put the ashtray down.

The Calm

I WAS getting a haircut. I was in the chair and three men were sitting along the wall across from me. Two of the men waiting I'd never seen before. But one of them I recognized, though I couldn't exactly place him. I kept looking at him as the barber worked on my hair. The man was moving a toothpick around in his mouth, a heavyset man, short wavy hair. And then I saw him in a cap and uniform, little eyes watchful in the lobby of a bank.

Of the other two, one was considerably the older, with a full head of curly gray hair. He was smoking. The third, though not so old, was nearly bald on top, but the hair at the sides hung over his ears. He had on logging boots, pants shiny with machine oil.

The barber put a hand on top of my head to turn me for a

better look. Then he said to the guard, "Did you get your deer, Charles?"

I liked this barber. We weren't acquainted well enough to call each other by name. But when I came in for a haircut, he knew me. He knew I used to fish. So we'd talk fishing. I don't think he hunted. But he could talk on any subject. In this regard, he was a good barber.

"Bill, it's a funny story. The damnedest thing," the guard said. He took out the toothpick and laid it in the ashtray. He shook his head. "I did and I didn't. So yes and no to your question."

I didn't like the man's voice. For a guard, the voice didn't fit. It wasn't the voice you'd expect.

The two other men looked up. The older man was turning the pages of a magazine, smoking, and the other fellow was holding a newspaper. They put down what they were looking at and turned to listen to the guard.

"Go on, Charles," the barber said. "Let's hear it."

The barber turned my head again, and went back to work with his clippers.

"WE were up on Fikle Ridge. My old man and me and the kid. We were hunting those draws. My old man was stationed at the head of one, and me and the kid were at the head of another. The kid had a hangover, goddamn his hide. The kid, he was green around the gills and drank water all day, mine and his both. It was in the afternoon and we'd been out since daybreak. But we had our hopes. We figured the hunters down below would move a deer in our direction. So we were sitting behind a log and watching the draw when we heard this shooting down in the valley."

"There's orchards down there," said the fellow with the newspaper. He was fidgeting a lot and kept crossing a leg, swinging his boot for a time, and then crossing his legs the other way. "Those deer hang out around those orchards."

"That's right," said the guard. "They'll go in there at night, the bastards, and eat those little green apples. Well, we heard this shooting and we're just sitting there on our hands when this big old buck comes up out of the underbrush not a hundred feet away. The kid sees him the same time I do, of course, and he throws down and starts banging. The knothead. That old buck wasn't in any danger. Not from the kid, as it turns out. But he can't tell where the shots are coming from. He doesn't know which way to jump. Then I get off a shot. But in all the commotion, I just stun him."

"Stunned him?" the barber said.

"You know, stun him," the guard said. "It was a gut shot. It just like stuns him. So he drops his head and begins this trembling. He trembles all over. The kid's still shooting. Me, I felt like I was back in Korea. So I shot again but missed. Then old Mr. Buck moves back into the brush. But now, by God, he doesn't have any oompf left in him. The kid has emptied his goddamn gun all to no purpose. But I hit solid. I'd rammed one right in his guts. That's what I meant by stunned him."

"Then what?" said the fellow with the newspaper, who had rolled it and was tapping it against his knee. "Then what? You must have trailed him. They find a hard place to die every time."

"But you trailed him?" the older man asked, though it wasn't really a question.

"I did. Me and the kid, we trailed him. But the kid wasn't good for much. He gets sick on the trail, slows us down. That chucklehead." The guard had to laugh now, thinking about that situation. "Drinking beer and chasing all night, then saying he can hunt deer. He knows better now, by God. But, sure, we trailed him. A good trail, too. Blood on the ground and blood on the leaves. Blood everywhere. Never seen a buck with so much blood. I don't know how the sucker kept going."

"Sometimes they'll go forever," the fellow with the newspaper said. "They find them a hard place to die every time."

"I chewed the kid out for missing his shot, and when he smarted off at me, I cuffed him a good one. Right here." The guard pointed to the side of his head and grinned. "I boxed his goddamn ears for him, that goddamn kid. He's not too old. He needed it. So the point is, it got too dark to trail, what with the kid laying back to vomit and all."

"Well, the coyotes will have that deer by now," the fellow with the newspaper said. "Them and the crows and the buzzards."

He unrolled the newspaper, smoothed it all the way out, and put it off to one side. He crossed a leg again. He looked around at the rest of us and shook his head.

The older man had turned in his chair and was looking out the window. He lit a cigarette.

"I figure so," the guard said. "Pity too. He was a big old son of a bitch. So in answer to your question, Bill, I both got my deer and I didn't. But we had venison on the table anyway. Because it turns out the old man has got himself a little spike in the meantime. Already has him back to camp, hanging up and gutted slick as a whistle, liver, heart, and kidneys wrapped in waxed paper and already setting in the cooler. A spike. Just a little bastard. But the old man, he was tickled."

The guard looked around the shop as if remembering. Then he picked up his toothpick and stuck it back in his mouth.

The older man put his cigarette out and turned to the guard. He drew a breath and said, "You ought to be out there right now looking for that deer instead of in here getting a haircut."

"You can't talk like that," the guard said. "You old fart. I've seen you someplace."

"I've seen you too," the old fellow said.

"Boys, that's enough. This is my barbershop," the barber said.

"I ought to box *your* ears," the old fellow said.

"You ought to try it," the guard said.

"Charles," the barber said.

The barber put his comb and scissors on the counter and his hands on my shoulders, as if he thought I was thinking to spring from the chair into the middle of it. "Albert, I've been cutting Charles's head of hair, and his boy's too, for years now. I wish you wouldn't pursue this."

The barber looked from one man to the other and kept his hands on my shoulders.

"Take it outside," the fellow with the newspaper said, flushed and hoping for something.

"That'll be enough," the barber said. "Charles, I don't want to hear anything more on the subject. Albert, you're next in line. Now." The barber turned to the fellow with the newspaper. "I don't know you from Adam, mister, but I'd appreciate if you wouldn't put your oar in."

THE guard got up. He said, "I think I'll come back for my cut later. Right now the company leaves something to be desired."

The guard went out and pulled the door closed, hard.

The old fellow sat smoking his cigarette. He looked out the window. He examined something on the back of his hand. He got up and put on his hat.

"I'm sorry, Bill," the old fellow said. "I can go a few more days."

"That's all right, Albert," the barber said.

When the old fellow went out, the barber stepped over to the window to watch him go.

"Albert's about dead from emphysema," the barber said from the window. "We used to fish together. He taught me salmon inside out. The women. They used to crawl all over that old boy. He's picked up a temper, though. But in all honesty, there was provocation."

The man with the newspaper couldn't sit still. He was on his feet and moving around, stopping to examine everything, the hat rack, the photos of Bill and his friends, the calendar from the hardware showing scenes for each month of the year. He flipped every page. He even went so far as to stand and scrutinize Bill's barbering license, which was up on the wall in a frame. Then he turned and said, "I'm going too," and out he went just like he said.

"Well, do you want me to finish barbering this hair or not?" the barber said to me as if I was the cause of everything.

THE barber turned me in the chair to face the mirror. He put a hand to either side of my head. He positioned me a last time, and then he brought his head down next to mine.

We looked into the mirror together, his hands still framing my head.

I was looking at myself, and he was looking at me too. But if the barber saw something, he didn't offer comment.

He ran his fingers through my hair. He did it slowly, as if thinking about something else. He ran his fingers through my hair. He did it tenderly, as a lover would.

That was in Crescent City, California, up near the Oregon border. I left soon after. But today I was thinking of that place, of Crescent City, and of how I was trying out a new life there with my wife, and how, in the barber's chair that morning, I had made up my mind to go. I was thinking today about the calm I felt when I closed my eyes and let the barber's fingers move through my hair, the sweetness of those fingers, the hair already starting to grow.

Popular Mechanics

EARLY that day the weather turned and the snow was melting into dirty water. Streaks of it ran down from the little shoulder-high window that faced the backyard. Cars slushed by on the street outside, where it was getting dark. But it was getting dark on the inside too.

He was in the bedroom pushing clothes into a suitcase when she came to the door.

I'm glad you're leaving! I'm glad you're leaving! she said. Do you hear?

He kept on putting his things into the suitcase.

Son of a bitch! I'm so glad you're leaving! She began to cry. You can't even look me in the face, can you?

Then she noticed the baby's picture on the bed and picked it up.

He looked at her and she wiped her eyes and stared at him before turning and going back to the living room.

Bring that back, he said.

Just get your things and get out, she said.

He did not answer. He fastened the suitcase, put on his coat, looked around the bedroom before turning off the light. Then he went out to the living room.

She stood in the doorway of the little kitchen, holding the baby.

I want the baby, he said.

Are you crazy?

No, but I want the baby. I'll get someone to come by for his things.

You're not touching this baby, she said.

The baby had begun to cry and she uncovered the blanket from around his head.

Oh, oh, she said, looking at the baby.

He moved toward her.

For God's sake! she said. She took a step back into the kitchen.

I want the baby.

Get out of here!

She turned and tried to hold the baby over in a corner behind the stove.

But he came up. He reached across the stove and tightened his hands on the baby.

Let go of him, he said.

Get away, get away! she cried.

The baby was red-faced and screaming. In the scuffle they knocked down a flowerpot that hung behind the stove.

He crowded her into the wall then, trying to break her grip. He held on to the baby and pushed with all his weight.

Let go of him, he said.

Don't, she said. You're hurting the baby, she said.

I'm not hurting the baby, he said.

The kitchen window gave no light. In the near-dark he worked on her fisted fingers with one hand and with the other hand he gripped the screaming baby up under an arm near the shoulder.

She felt her fingers being forced open. She felt the baby going from her.

No! she screamed just as her hands came loose.

She would have it, this baby. She grabbed for the baby's other arm. She caught the baby around the wrist and leaned back.

But he would not let go. He felt the baby slipping out of his hands and he pulled back very hard.

In this manner, the issue was decided.

Everything Stuck to Him

SHE'S in Milan for Christmas and wants to know what it was like when she was a kid.

Tell me, she says. Tell me what it was like when I was a kid. She sips Strega, waits, eyes him closely.

She is a cool, slim, attractive girl, a survivor from top to bottom.

That was a long time ago. That was twenty years ago, he says.

You can remember, she says. Go on.

What do you want to hear? he says. What else can I tell you? I could tell you about something that happened when you were a baby. It involves you, he says. But only in a minor way.

Tell me, she says. But first fix us another so you won't have to stop in the middle.

He comes back from the kitchen with drinks, settles into his chair, begins.

THEY were kids themselves, but they were crazy in love, this eighteen-year-old boy and this seventeen-year-old girl when they married. Not all that long afterwards they had a daughter.

The baby came along in late November during a cold spell that just happened to coincide with the peak of the waterfowl season. The boy loved to hunt, you see. That's part of it.

The boy and girl, husband and wife, father and mother, they lived in a little apartment under a dentist's office. Each night they cleaned the dentist's place upstairs in exchange for rent and utilities. In summer they were expected to maintain the lawn and the flowers. In winter the boy shoveled snow and spread rock salt on the walks. Are you still with me? Are you getting the picture?

I am, she says.

That's good, he says. So one day the dentist finds out they were using his letterhead for their personal correspondence. But that's another story.

He gets up from his chair and looks out the window. He sees the tile rooftops and the snow that is falling steadily on them.

Tell the story, she says.

The two kids were very much in love. On top of this they had great ambitions. They were always talking about the things they were going to do and the places they were going to go.

Now the boy and girl slept in the bedroom, and the baby slept in the living room. Let's say the baby was about three months old and had only just begun to sleep through the night.

On this one Saturday night after finishing his work upstairs, the boy stayed in the dentist's office and called an old hunting friend of his father's.

Carl, he said when the man picked up the receiver, believe it or not, I'm a father.

Congratulations, Carl said. How is the wife?

She's fine, Carl. Everybody's fine.

That's good, Carl said, I'm glad to hear it. But if you called about going hunting, I'll tell you something. The geese are flying to beat the band. I don't think I've ever seen so many. Got five today. Going back in the morning, so come along if you want to.

I want to, the boy said.

The boy hung up the telephone and went downstairs to tell the girl. She watched while he laid out his things. Hunting coat, shell bag, boots, socks, hunting cap, long underwear, pump gun.

What time will you be back? the girl said.

Probably around noon, the boy said. But maybe as late as six o'clock. Would that be too late?

It's fine, she said. The baby and I will get along fine. You go and have some fun. When you get back, we'll dress the baby up and go visit Sally.

The boy said, Sounds like a good idea.

Sally was the girl's sister. She was striking. I don't know if you've seen pictures of her. The boy was a little in love with Sally, just as he was a little in love with Betsy, who was another sister the girl had. The boy used to say to the girl, If we weren't married, I could go for Sally.

What about Betsy? the girl used to say. I hate to admit it, but I truly feel she's better looking than Sally and me. What about Betsy?

Betsy too, the boy used to say.

AFTER dinner he turned up the furnace and helped her bathe the baby. He marveled again at the infant who had half his features and half the girl's. He powdered the tiny body. He powdered between fingers and toes.

He emptied the bath into the sink and went upstairs to check the air. It was overcast and cold. The grass, what there was of it, looked like canvas, stiff and gray under the street light.

Snow lay in piles beside the walk. A car went by. He heard sand under the tires. He let himself imagine what it might be like tomorrow, geese beating the air over his head, shotgun plunging against his shoulder.

Then he locked the door and went downstairs.

In bed they tried to read. But both of them fell asleep, she first, letting the magazine sink to the quilt.

IT was the baby's cries that woke him up.

The light was on out there, and the girl was standing next to the crib rocking the baby in her arms. She put the baby down, turned out the light, and came back to the bed.

He heard the baby cry. This time the girl stayed where

she was. The baby cried fitfully and stopped. The boy listened, then dozed. But the baby's cries woke him again. The living room light was burning. He sat up and turned on the lamp.

I don't know what's wrong, the girl said, walking back and forth with the baby. I've changed her and fed her, but she keeps on crying. I'm so tired I'm afraid I might drop her.

You come back to bed, the boy said. I'll hold her for a while.

He got up and took the baby, and the girl went to lie down again.

Just rock her for a few minutes, the girl said from the bedroom. Maybe she'll go back to sleep.

The boy sat on the sofa and held the baby. He jiggled it in his lap until he got its eyes to close, his own eyes closing right along. He rose carefully and put the baby back in the crib.

It was a quarter to four, which gave him forty-five minutes. He crawled into bed and dropped off. But a few minutes later the baby was crying again, and this time they both got up.

The boy did a terrible thing. He swore.

For God's sake, what's the matter with you? the girl said to the boy. Maybe she's sick or something. Maybe we shouldn't have given her the bath.

The boy picked up the baby. The baby kicked its feet and smiled.

Look, the boy said, I really don't think there's anything wrong with her.

How do you know that? the girl said. Here, let me have her. I know I ought to give her something, but I don't know what it's supposed to be.

The girl put the baby down again. The boy and the girl

looked at the baby, and the baby began to cry.

The girl took the baby. Baby, baby, the girl said with tears in her eyes.

Probably it's something on her stomach, the boy said.

The girl didn't answer. She went on rocking the baby, paying no attention to the boy.

THE boy waited. He went to the kitchen and put on water for coffee. He drew his woolen underwear on over his shorts and T-shirt, buttoned up, then got into his clothes.

What are you doing? the girl said.

Going hunting, the boy said.

I don't think you should, she said. I don't want to be left alone with her like this.

Carl's planning on me going, the boy said. We've planned it.

I don't care about what you and Carl planned, she said. And I don't care about Carl, either. I don't even know Carl.

You've met Carl before. You know him, the boy said. What do you mean you don't know him?

That's not the point and you know it, the girl said.

What is the point? the boy said. The point is we planned it.

The girl said, I'm your wife. This is your baby. She's sick or something. Look at her. Why else is she crying?

I know you're my wife, the boy said.

The girl began to cry. She put the baby back in the crib. But the baby started up again. The girl dried her eyes on the sleeve of her nightgown and picked the baby up.

THE boy laced up his boots. He put on his shirt, his sweater, his coat. The kettle whistled on the stove in the kitchen.

You're going to have to choose, the girl said. Carl or us. I mean it.

What do you mean? the boy said.

You heard what I said, the girl said. If you want a family, you're going to have to choose.

They stared at each other. Then the boy took up his hunting gear and went outside. He started the car. He went around to the car windows and, making a job of it, scraped away the ice.

He turned off the motor and sat awhile. And then he got out and went back inside.

The living-room light was on. The girl was asleep on the bed. The baby was asleep beside her.

The boy took off his boots. Then he took off everything else. In his socks and his long underwear, he sat on the sofa and read the Sunday paper.

The girl and the baby slept on. After a while, the boy went to the kitchen and started frying bacon.

The girl came out in her robe and put her arms around the boy.

Hey, the boy said.

I'm sorry, the girl said.

It's all right, the boy said.

I didn't mean to snap like that.

It was my fault, he said.

You sit down, the girl said. How does a waffle sound with bacon?

Sounds great, the boy said.

She took the bacon out of the pan and made waffle batter. He sat at the table and watched her move around the kitchen.

She put a plate in front of him with bacon, a waffle. He spread butter and poured syrup. But when he started to cut, he turned the plate into his lap.

I don't believe it, he said, jumping up from the table.

If you could see yourself, the girl said.

The boy looked down at himself, at everything stuck to his underwear.

I was starved, he said, shaking his head.

You were starved, she said, laughing.

He peeled off the woolen underwear and threw it at the bathroom door. Then he opened his arms and the girl moved into them.

We won't fight anymore, she said.

The boy said, We won't.

HE gets up from his chair and refills their glasses.

That's it, he says. End of story. I admit it's not much of a story.

I was interested, she says.

He shrugs and carries his drink over to the window. It's dark now but still snowing.

Things change, he says. I don't know how they do. But they do without your realizing it or wanting them to.

Yes, that's true, only— But she does not finish what she started.

She drops the subject. In the window's reflection he sees her study her nails. Then she raises her head. Speaking brightly, she asks if he is going to show her the city, after all.

He says, Put your boots on and let's go.

But he stays by the window, remembering. They had laughed. They had leaned on each other and laughed until the tears had come, while everything else—the cold, and where he'd go in it—was outside, for a while anyway.

What We Talk About When We Talk About Love

MY friend Mel McGinnis was talking. Mel McGinnis is a cardiologist, and sometimes that gives him the right.

The four of us were sitting around his kitchen table drinking gin. Sunlight filled the kitchen from the big window behind the sink. There were Mel and me and his second wife, Teresa—Terri, we called her—and my wife, Laura. We lived in Albuquerque then. But we were all from somewhere else.

There was an ice bucket on the table. The gin and the tonic water kept going around, and we somehow got on the subject of love. Mel thought real love was nothing less than spiritual love. He said he'd spent five years in a seminary before quitting to go to medical school. He said he still looked back on those years in the seminary as the most important years in his life.

Terri said the man she lived with before she lived with Mel loved her so much he tried to kill her. Then Terri said, "He beat me up one night. He dragged me around the living room by my ankles. He kept saying, 'I love you, I love you, you bitch.' He went on dragging me around the living room. My head kept knocking on things." Terri looked around the table. "What do you do with love like that?"

She was a bone-thin woman with a pretty face, dark eyes, and brown hair that hung down her back. She liked necklaces made of turquoise, and long pendant earrings.

"My God, don't be silly. That's not love, and you know it," Mel said. "I don't know what you'd call it, but I sure know you wouldn't call it love."

"Say what you want to, but I know it was," Terri said. "It may sound crazy to you, but it's true just the same. People are different, Mel. Sure, sometimes he may have acted crazy. Okay. But he loved me. In his own way maybe, but he loved me. There was love there, Mel. Don't say there wasn't."

Mel let out his breath. He held his glass and turned to Laura and me. "The man threatened to kill me," Mel said. He finished his drink and reached for the gin bottle. "Terri's a romantic. Terri's of the kick-me-so-I'll-know-you-love-me school. Terri, hon, don't look that way." Mel reached across the table and touched Terri's cheek with his fingers. He grinned at her.

"Now he wants to make up," Terri said.

"Make up what?" Mel said. "What is there to make up? I know what I know. That's all."

"How'd we get started on this subject, anyway?" Terri said. She raised her glass and drank from it. "Mel always has love on his mind," she said. "Don't you, honey?" She smiled. and I thought that was the last of it.

"I just wouldn't call Ed's behavior love. That's all I'm saying, honey," Mel said. "What about you guys?" Mel said to Laura and me. "Does that sound like love to you?"

"I'm the wrong person to ask," I said. "I didn't even know the man. I've only heard his name mentioned in passing. I wouldn't know. You'd have to know the particulars. But I think what you're saying is that love is an absolute."

Mel said, "The kind of love I'm talking about is. The kind of love I'm talking about, you don't try to kill people."

Laura said, "I don't know anything about Ed, or anything about the situation. But who can judge anyone else's situation?"

I touched the back of Laura's hand. She gave me a quick smile. I picked up Laura's hand. It was warm, the nails polished, perfectly manicured. I encircled the broad wrist with my fingers, and I held her.

"WHEN I left, he drank rat poison," Terri said. She clasped her arms with her hands. "They took him to the hospital in Santa Fe. That's where we lived then, about ten miles out. They saved his life. But his gums went crazy from it. I mean they pulled away from his teeth. After that, his teeth stood out like fangs. My God," Terri said. She waited a minute, then let go of her arms and picked up her glass.

"What people won't do!" Laura said.

"He's out of the action now," Mel said. "He's dead."

Mel handed me the saucer of limes. I took a section, squeezed it over my drink, and stirred the ice cubes with my finger.

"It gets worse," Terri said. "He shot himself in the mouth. But he bungled that too. Poor Ed," she said. Terri shook her head.

"Poor Ed nothing," Mel said. "He was dangerous."

Mel was forty-five years old. He was tall and rangy with curly soft hair. His face and arms were brown from the tennis he played. When he was sober, his gestures, all his movements, were precise, very careful.

"He did love me though, Mel. Grant me that," Terri said. "That's all I'm asking. He didn't love me the way you love me. I'm not saying that. But he loved me. You can grant me that, can't you?"

"What do you mean, he bungled it?" I said.

Laura leaned forward with her glass. She put her elbows on the table and held her glass in both hands. She glanced from Mel to Terri and waited with a look of bewilderment on her open face, as if amazed that such things happened to people you were friendly with.

"How'd he bungle it when he killed himself?" I said.

"I'll tell you what happened," Mel said. "He took this twenty-two pistol he'd bought to threaten Terri and me with. Oh, I'm serious, the man was always threatening. You should have seen the way we lived in those days. Like fugitives. I even bought a gun myself. Can you believe it? A guy like me? But I did. I bought one for self-defense and carried it in the glove compartment. Sometimes I'd have to leave the apartment in the middle of the night. To go to the hospital, you know? Terri and I weren't married then, and my first wife had the house and kids, the dog, everything, and Terri and I were living in this apartment here. Sometimes, as I say, I'd get a call in the middle of the night and have to go in to the hospital at two or three in the morning. It'd be dark out there in the parking lot, and I'd break into a sweat before I could even get to my car. I never knew if he was going to come up out of the shrubbery or from behind a car and start shooting. I mean, the man was crazy. He was capable of wiring a bomb, anything. He used to call my service at all hours and say he needed to talk to the doctor, and when I'd return the call, he'd say, 'Son of a bitch, your days are numbered.' Little things like that. It was scary, I'm telling you."

"I still feel sorry for him," Terri said.

"It sounds like a nightmare," Laura said. "But what exactly happened after he shot himself?"

Laura is a legal secretary. We'd met in a professional capacity. Before we knew it, it was a courtship. She's thirty-five, three years younger than I am. In addition to being in love, we like each other and enjoy one another's company. She's easy to be with.

"WHAT happened?" Laura said.

Mel said, "He shot himself in the mouth in his room. Someone heard the shot and told the manager. They came in with a passkey, saw what had happened, and called an ambulance. I happened to be there when they brought him in, alive but past recall. The man lived for three days. His head swelled up to twice the size of a normal head. I'd never seen anything like it, and I hope I never do again. Terri wanted to go in and sit with him when she found out about it. We had a fight over it. I didn't think she should see him like that. I didn't think she should see him, and I still don't."

"Who won the fight?" Laura said.

"I was in the room with him when he died," Terri said. "He never came up out of it. But I sat with him. He didn't have anyone else."

"He was dangerous," Mel said. "If you call that love, you can have it."

"It was love," Terri said. "Sure, it's abnormal in most people's eyes. But he was willing to die for it. He did die for it."

"I sure as hell wouldn't call it love," Mel said. "I mean, no one knows what he did it for. I've seen a lot of suicides, and I couldn't say anyone ever knew what they did it for."

Mel put his hands behind his neck and tilted his chair back. "I'm not interested in that kind of love," he said. "If that's love, you can have it."

Terri said, "We were afraid. Mel even made a will out and wrote to his brother in California who used to be a Green Beret. Mel told him who to look for if something happened to him."

Terri drank from her glass. She said, "But Mel's right—we lived like fugitives. We were afraid. Mel was, weren't you, honey? I even called the police at one point, but they were no help. They said they couldn't do anything until Ed actually did something. Isn't that a laugh?" Terri said.

She poured the last of the gin into her glass and waggled the bottle. Mel got up from the table and went to the cupboard. He took down another bottle.

"WELL, Nick and I know what love is," Laura said. "For us, I mean," Laura said. She bumped my knee with her knee. "You're supposed to say something now," Laura said, and turned her smile on me.

For an answer, I took Laura's hand and raised it to my lips. I made a big production out of kissing her hand. Everyone was amused.

"We're lucky," I said.

"You guys," Terri said. "Stop that now. You're making me sick. You're still on the honeymoon, for God's sake. You're still gaga, for crying out loud. Just wait. How long have you been together now? How long has it been? A year? Longer than a year?"

"Going on a year and a half," Laura said, flushed and smiling.

"Oh, now," Terri said. "Wait awhile."

She held her drink and gazed at Laura.

"I'm only kidding," Terri said.

Mel opened the gin and went around the table with the bottle.

"Here, you guys," he said. "Let's have a toast. I want to propose a toast. A toast to love. To true love," Mel said.

We touched glasses.

"To love," we said.

OUTSIDE in the backyard, one of the dogs began to bark. The leaves of the aspen that leaned past the window ticked against the glass. The afternoon sun was like a presence in this room, the spacious light of ease and generosity. We could have been anywhere, somewhere enchanted. We raised our glasses again and grinned at each other like children who had agreed on something forbidden.

"I'll tell you what real love is," Mel said. "I mean, I'll give you a good example. And then you can draw your own conclusions." He poured more gin into his glass. He added an ice cube and a sliver of lime. We waited and sipped our drinks. Laura and I touched knees again. I put a hand on her warm thigh and left it there.

"What do any of us really know about love?" Mel said. "It seems to me we're just beginners at love. We say we love each other and we do, I don't doubt it. I love Terri and Terri loves me, and you guys love each other too. You know the kind of love I'm talking about now. Physical love, that impulse that drives you to someone special, as well as love of the other person's being, his or her essence, as it were. Carnal love and, well, call it sentimental love, the day-to-day caring about the other person. But sometimes I have a hard time accounting for the fact that I must have loved my first wife too. But I did, I know I did. So I suppose I am like Terri in that regard. Terri and Ed." He thought about it and then he went on. "There was a time when I thought I loved my first wife more than life itself. But now I hate her guts. I do. How do you explain that? What happened to that love? What happened to it, is what I'd like to know. I wish someone could tell me. Then there's Ed. Okay, we're back to Ed. He loves Terri so much he tries to kill her and he winds up killing himself." Mel stopped talking and swallowed from his glass. "You guys have been together eighteen months and you love each other. It shows all over you. You glow with it. But you both loved other people before you met each other. You've both been married before, just like us. And you probably loved other people before that too, even. Terri and I have been together five years, been married for four. And the terrible thing, the terrible thing is, but the good thing too, the saving grace, you might say, is that if something happened to one of us—excuse me for saying this—but if something happened to one of us tomorrow, I think the other one, the other person, would grieve for a while, you know, but then the surviving party would go out and love again, have someone else soon enough. All this, all of this love we're talking about, it would just be a memory. Maybe not even a memory. Am I wrong? Am I way off base? Because I want you to set me straight if you think I'm wrong. I want to know. I mean, I don't know anything, and I'm the first one to admit it."

"Mel, for God's sake," Terri said. She reached out and took hold of his wrist. "Are you getting drunk? Honey? Are you drunk?"

"Honey, I'm just talking," Mel said. "All right? I don't have to be drunk to say what I think. I mean, we're all just talking, right?" Mel said. He fixed his eyes on her.

"Sweetie, I'm not criticizing," Terri said.

She picked up her glass.

"I'm not on call today," Mel said. "Let me remind you of that. I am not on call," he said.

"Mel, we love you," Laura said.

Mel looked at Laura. He looked at her as if he could not

place her, as if she was not the woman she was.

"Love you too, Laura," Mel said. "And you, Nick, love you too. You know something?" Mel said. "You guys are our pals," Mel said.

He picked up his glass.

MEL said, "I was going to tell you about something. I mean, I was going to prove a point. You see, this happened a few months ago, but it's still going on right now, and it ought to make us feel ashamed when we talk like we know what we're talking about when we talk about love."

"Come on now," Terri said. "Don't talk like you're drunk if you're not drunk."

"Just shut up for once in your life," Mel said very quietly. "Will you do me a favor and do that for a minute? So as I was saying, there's this old couple who had this car wreck out on the interstate. A kid hit them and they were all torn to shit and nobody was giving them much chance to pull through."

Terri looked at us and then back at Mel. She seemed anxious, or maybe that's too strong a word.

Mel was handing the bottle around the table.

"I was on call that night," Mel said. "It was May or maybe it was June. Terri and I had just sat down to dinner when the hospital called. There'd been this thing out on the interstate. Drunk kid, teenager, plowed his dad's pickup into this camper with this old couple in it. They were up in their mid-seventies, that couple. The kid—eighteen, nineteen, something—he was DOA. Taken the steering wheel through his sternum. The old couple, they were alive, you understand. I mean, just barely. But they had everything.

Multiple fractures, internal injuries, hemorrhaging, contusions, lacerations, the works, and they each of them had themselves concussions. They were in a bad way, believe me. And, of course, their age was two strikes against them. I'd say she was worse off than he was. Ruptured spleen along with everything else. Both kneecaps broken. But they'd been wearing their seatbelts and, God knows, that's what saved them for the time being."

"Folks, this is an advertisement for the National Safety Council," Terri said. "This is your spokesman, Dr. Melvin R. McGinnis, talking." Terri laughed. "Mel," she said, "sometimes you're just too much. But I love you, hon," she said.

"Honey, I love you," Mel said.

He leaned across the table. Terri met him halfway. They kissed.

"Terri's right," Mel said as he settled himself again. "Get those seatbelts on. But seriously, they were in some shape, those oldsters. By the time I got down there, the kid was dead, as I said. He was off in a corner, laid out on a gurney. I took one look at the old couple and told the ER nurse to get me a neurologist and an orthopedic man and a couple of surgeons down there right away."

He drank from his glass. "I'll try to keep this short," he said. "So we took the two of them up to the OR and worked like fuck on them most of the night. They had these incredible reserves, those two. You see that once in a while. So we did everything that could be done, and toward morning we're giving them a fifty-fifty chance, maybe less than that for her. So here they are, still alive the next morning. So, okay, we move them into the ICU, which is where they both kept plugging away at it for two weeks, hitting it better and better on all the scopes. So we transfer them out to their own room."

Mel stopped talking. "Here," he said, "let's drink this cheapo gin the hell up. Then we're going to dinner, right? Terri and I know a new place. That's where we'll go, to this new place we know about. But we're not going until we finish up this cut-rate, lousy gin."

Terri said, "We haven't actually eaten there yet. But it looks good. From the outside, you know."

"I like food," Mel said. "If I had it to do all over again, I'd be a chef, you know? Right, Terri?" Mel said.

He laughed. He fingered the ice in his glass.

"Terri knows," he said. "Terri can tell you. But let me say this. If I could come back again in a different life, a different time and all, you know what? I'd like to come back as a knight. You were pretty safe wearing all that armor. It was all right being a knight until gunpowder and muskets and pistols came along."

"Mel would like to ride a horse and carry a lance," Terri said.

"Carry a woman's scarf with you everywhere," Laura said.

"Or just a woman," Mel said.

"Shame on you," Laura said.

Terri said, "Suppose you came back as a serf. The serfs didn't have it so good in those days," Terri said.

"The serfs never had it good," Mel said. "But I guess even the knights were vessels to someone. Isn't that the way it worked? But then everyone is always a vessel to someone. Isn't that right? Terri? But what I liked about knights, besides their ladies, was that they had that suit of armor, you know, and they couldn't get hurt very easy. No cars in those days, you know? No drunk teenagers to tear into your ass."

"VASSALS," Terri said.

"What?" Mel said.

"Vassals," Terri said. "They were called vassals, not vessels."

"Vassals, vessels," Mel said, "what the fuck's the difference? You knew what I meant anyway. All right," Mel said. "So I'm not educated. I learned my stuff. I'm a heart surgeon, sure, but I'm just a mechanic. I go in and I fuck around and I fix things. Shit," Mel said.

"Modesty doesn't become you," Terri said.

"He's just a humble sawbones," I said. "But sometimes they suffocated in all that armor, Mel. They'd even have heart attacks if it got too hot and they were too tired and worn out. I read somewhere that they'd fall off their horses and not be able to get up because they were too tired to stand with all that armor on them. They got trampled by their own horses sometimes."

"That's terrible," Mel said. "That's a terrible thing, Nicky. I guess they'd just lay there and wait until somebody came along and made a shish kebab out of them."

"Some other vessel," Terri said.

"That's right," Mel said. "Some vassal would come along and spear the bastard in the name of love. Or whatever the fuck it was they fought over in those days."

"Same things we fight over these days," Terri said.

Laura said, "Nothing's changed."

The color was still high in Laura's cheeks. Her eyes were bright. She brought her glass to her lips.

Mel poured himself another drink. He looked at the label closely as if studying a long row of numbers. Then he slowly put the bottle down on the table and slowly reached for the tonic water.

"WHAT about the old couple?" Laura said. "You didn't finish that story you started."

Laura was having a hard time lighting her cigarette. Her matches kept going out.

The sunshine inside the room was different now, changing, getting thinner. But the leaves outside the window were still shimmering, and I stared at the pattern they made on the panes and on the Formica counter. They weren't the same patterns, of course.

"What about the old couple?" I said.

"Older but wiser," Terri said.

Mel stared at her.

Terri said, "Go on with your story, hon. I was only kidding. Then what happened?"

"Terri, sometimes," Mel said.

"Please, Mel," Terri said. "Don't always be so serious, sweetie. Can't you take a joke?"

"Where's the joke?" Mel said.

He held his glass and gazed steadily at his wife.

"What happened?" Laura said.

Mel fastened his eyes on Laura. He said, "Laura, if I didn't have Terri and if I didn't love her so much, and if Nick wasn't my best friend, I'd fall in love with you. I'd carry you off, honey," he said.

"Tell your story," Terri said. "Then we'll go to that new place, okay?"

"Okay," Mel said. "Where was I?" he said. He stared at the table and then he began again.

"I dropped in to see each of them every day, sometimes twice a day if I was up doing other calls anyway. Casts and bandages, head to foot, the both of them. You know, you've seen it in the movies. That's just the way they looked, just like in the movies. Little eye-holes and nose-holes and mouth-holes. And she had to have her legs slung up on top of it. Well, the husband was very depressed for the longest while. Even after he found out that his wife was going to pull through, he was still very depressed. Not about the accident, though. I mean, the accident was one thing, but it wasn't everything. I'd get up to his mouth-hole, you know, and he'd say no, it wasn't the accident exactly but it was because he couldn't see her through his eye-holes. He said that was what was making him feel so bad. Can you imagine? I'm telling you, the man's heart was breaking because he couldn't turn his goddamn head and *see* his goddamn wife."

Mel looked around the table and shook his head at what he was going to say.

"I mean, it was killing the old fart just because he couldn't *look* at the fucking woman."

We all looked at Mel.

"Do you see what I'm saying?" he said.

MAYBE we were a little drunk by then. I know it was hard keeping things in focus. The light was draining out of the room, going back through the window where it had come from. Yet nobody made a move to get up from the table to turn on the overhead light.

"Listen," Mel said. "Let's finish this fucking gin. There's about enough left here for one shooter all around. Then let's go eat. Let's go to the new place."

"He's depressed," Terri said. "Mel, why don't you take a pill?"

Mel shook his head. "I've taken everything there is."

"We all need a pill now and then," I said.

"Some people are born needing them," Terri said.

She was using her finger to rub at something on the table. Then she stopped rubbing.

"I think I want to call my kids," Mel said. "Is that all right with everybody? I'll call my kids," he said.

Terri said, "What if Marjorie answers the phone? You guys, you've heard us on the subject of Marjorie? Honey, you know you don't want to talk to Marjorie. It'll make you feel even worse."

"I don't want to talk to Marjorie," Mel said. "But I want to talk to my kids."

"There isn't a day goes by that Mel doesn't say he wishes she'd get married again. Or else die," Terri said. "For one thing," Terri said, "she's bankrupting us. Mel says it's just to spite him that she won't get married again. She has a boyfriend who lives with her and the kids, so Mel is supporting the boyfriend too."

"She's allergic to bees," Mel said. "If I'm not praying she'll get married again, I'm praying she'll get herself stung to death by a swarm of fucking bees."

"Shame on you," Laura said.

"Bzzzzzzz," Mel said, turning his fingers into bees and buzzing them at Terri's throat. Then he let his hands drop all the way to his sides.

"She's vicious," Mel said. "Sometimes I think I'll go up there dressed like a beekeeper. You know, that hat that's like a helmet with the plate that comes down over your face, the big gloves, and the padded coat? I'll knock on the door and let loose a hive of bees in the house. But first I'd make sure the kids were out, of course."

He crossed one leg over the other. It seemed to take him a lot of time to do it. Then he put both feet on the floor and leaned forward, elbows on the table, his chin cupped in his hands.

"Maybe I won't call the kids, after all. Maybe it isn't such a hot idea. Maybe we'll just go eat. How does that sound?"

"Sounds fine to me," I said. "Eat or not eat. Or keep drinking. I could head right on out into the sunset."

"What does that mean, honey?" Laura said.

"It just means what I said," I said. "It means I could just keep going. That's all it means."

"I could eat something myself," Laura said. "I don't think I've ever been so hungry in my life. Is there something to nibble on?"

"I'll put out some cheese and crackers," Terri said.

But Terri just sat there. She did not get up to get anything.

Mel turned his glass over. He spilled it out on the table.

"Gin's gone," Mel said.

Terri said, "Now what?"

I could hear my heart beating. I could hear everyone's heart. I could hear the human noise we sat there making, not one of us moving, not even when the room went dark.

One More Thing

L. D.'s wife, Maxine, told him to get out the night she came home from work and found L.D. drunk again and being abusive to Rae, their fifteen-year-old. L.D. and Rae were at the kitchen table, arguing. Maxine didn't have time to put her purse away or take off her coat.

Rae said, "Tell him, Mom. Tell him what we talked about."

L.D. turned the glass in his hand, but he didn't drink from it. Maxine had him in a fierce and disquieting gaze.

"Keep your nose out of things you don't know anything about," L.D. said. L.D. said, "I can't take anybody seriously who sits around all day reading astrology magazines."

"This has nothing to do with astrology," Rae said. "You don't have to insult me."

As for Rae, she hadn't been to school for weeks. She said no one could make her go. Maxine said it was another tragedy in a long line of low-rent tragedies.

"Why don't you both shut up!" Maxine said. "My God, I already have a headache."

"Tell him, Mom," Rae said. "Tell him it's all in his head. Anybody who knows anything about it will tell you that's where it is!"

"How about sugar diabetes?" L.D. said. "What about epilepsy? Can the brain control that?"

He raised the glass right under Maxine's eyes and finished his drink.

"Diabetes, too," Rae said. "Epilepsy. Anything! The brain is the most powerful organ in the body, for your information."

She picked up his cigarettes and lit one for herself.

"Cancer. What about cancer?" L.D. said.

He thought he might have her there. He looked at Maxine.

"I don't know how we got started on this," L.D. said to Maxine.

"Cancer," Rae said, and shook her head at his simplicity. "Cancer, too. Cancer *starts* in the brain."

"That's crazy!" L.D. said. He hit the table with the flat of his hand. The ashtray jumped. His glass fell on its side and rolled off. "You're crazy, Rae! Do you know that?"

"Shut up!" Maxine said.

She unbuttoned her coat and put her purse down on the counter. She looked at L.D. and said, "L.D., I've had it. So has Rae. So has everyone who knows you. I've been thinking it over. I want you out of here. Tonight. This minute. Now. Get the hell out of here right now."

L.D. had no intention of going anywhere. He looked from Maxine to the jar of pickles that had been on the table since lunch. He picked up the jar and pitched it through the kitchen window.

Rae jumped away from her chair. "God! He's crazy!"

She went to stand next to her mother. She took in little breaths through her mouth.

"Call the police," Maxine said. "He's violent. Get out of the kitchen before he hurts you. Call the police," Maxine said.

They started backing out of the kitchen.

"I'm going," L.D. said. "All right, I'm going right now," he said. "It suits me to a tee. You're nuts here, anyway. This is a nuthouse. There's another life out there. Believe me, this is no picnic, this nuthouse."

He could feel air from the hole in the window on his face.

"That's where I'm going," he said. "Out there," he said and pointed.

"Good," Maxine said.

"All right, I'm going," L.D. said.

He slammed down his hand on the table. He kicked back his chair. He stood up.

"You won't ever see me again," L.D. said.

"You've given me plenty to remember you by," Maxine said.

"Okay," L.D. said.

"Go on, get out," Maxine said. "I'm paying the rent here, and I'm saying go. Now."

"I'm going," he said. "Don't push me," he said. "I'm going."

"Just go," Maxine said.

"I'm leaving this nuthouse," L.D. said.

He made his way into the bedroom and took one of her suitcases from the closet. It was an old white Naugahyde suitcase with a broken clasp. She'd used to pack it full of sweater sets and carry it with her to college. He had gone to college too. He threw the suitcase onto the bed and began putting in his underwear, his trousers, his shirts, his sweaters, his old leather belt with the brass buckle, his socks, and everything else he had. From the nightstand he took magazines for reading material. He took the ashtray. He put everything he could into the suitcase, everything it could hold. He fastened the one good side, secured the strap, and then he remembered his bathroom things. He found the vinyl shaving bag up on the closet shelf behind her hats. Into it went his razor and his shaving cream, his talcum powder and his stick deodorant and his toothbrush. He took the toothpaste, too. And then he got the dental floss.

HE could hear them in the living room talking in their low voices.

He washed his face. He put the soap and towel into the shaving bag. Then he put in the soap dish and the glass from over the sink and the fingernail clippers and her eyelash curlers.

He couldn't get the shaving bag closed, but that was okay. He put on his coat and picked up the suitcase. He went into the living room.

When she saw him, Maxine put her arm around Rae's shoulders.

"This is it," L.D. said. "This is good-bye," he said. "I don't know what else to say except I guess I'll never see you again. You too," L.D. said to Rae. "You and your crackpot ideas."

"Go," Maxine said. She took Rae's hand. "Haven't you done enough damage in this house already? Go on, L.D. Get out of here and leave us in peace."

"Just remember," Rae said. "It's in your head."

"I'm going, that's all I can say," L.D. said. "Anyplace. Away from this nuthouse," he said. "That's the main thing."

He took a last look around the living room and then he moved the suitcase from one hand to the other and put the shaving bag under his arm. "I'll be in touch, Rae. Maxine, you're better off out of this nuthouse yourself."

"You made it into a nuthouse," Maxine said. "If it's a nuthouse, then that's what you made it."

He put the suitcase down and the shaving bag on top of the suitcase. He drew himself up and faced them.

They moved back.

"Watch it, Mom," Rae said.

"I'm not afraid of him," Maxine said.

L.D. put the shaving bag under his arm and picked up the suitcase.

He said, "I just want to say one more thing."

But then he could not think what it could possibly be.

ABOUT THE AUTHOR

Raymond Carver was born in Clatskanie, Oregon, in 1939, and lived in Port Angeles, Washington, until his death on August 2, 1988. He was a Guggenheim Fellow in 1979 and was twice awarded grants from the National Endowment for the Arts. In 1983 Carver received the prestigious Mildred and Harold Strauss Living Award, and in 1985 *Poetry* magazine's Levinson Prize. In 1988 he was elected to the American Academy and Institute of Arts and Letters and awarded a Doctorate of Letters from Hartford University. He received a Brandeis Citation in fiction for 1988. His work has been translated into more than twenty languages.

ALSO BY

RAYMOND CARVER

FICTION

CATHEDRAL

Twelve brilliant works of short fiction. "His stories possess an awesome, mesmerizing power. Out of the moments when good luck runs out, Carver makes the highest art."—Newsday

FIRES

The wide-ranging collection that reveals Carver's astonishing versatility as poet, essayist, and short-story writer. "He is one of the great short story writers of our time — of any time."—Philadelphia Inquirer

WHERE I'M CALLING FROM

The summation of a triumphant career. "[Carver's stories] can...be counted among the masterpieces of American fiction."—Irving Howe, The New York Times Book Review

POETRY

ULTRAMARINE

"Mr. Carver is heir to the most appealing American poetic voice....This book is a treasure, one to return to."—The New York Times

WHERE WATER COMES TOGETHER WITH OTHER WATER

"The most vigorous poems in this new collection function as distilled, heightened versions of his stories, offering us fugitive glimpses of ordinary lives on the edge."—The New York Times

Available at your local bookstore, or call toll-free to order 1-800-733-3000 (credit cards only).